This book belongs to

....

Grandma's
Special Recipes

Grandma's
Special Recipes

hinkler

Published by Hinkler Books Pty Ltd
45–55 Fairchild Street
Heatherton Victoria 3202 Australia
www.hinkler.com.au

hinkler

© A.C.N 144 619 894 (2011)
Cover and page design © Hinkler Books Pty Ltd 2011

Cover Design: Beverley Gutierrez
Stitching, embroidery and screen-printed illustrations created by Beverley Gutierrez
Internal Design: Beverley Gutierrez and Hinkler Design Studio
Cover and page 156, blueberry cheesecake © Foodcollection/STOCKFOOD AUSTRALIA
© Shutterstock.com: page 6, tool in the kitchen © Bernd Meiseberg;
page 36, baking ingredients © KAppleyard; page 66, antique terrine © vorkot;
page 90, teacup and saucer © 54613; page 124, still life on chopping board © eAlisa;
page 150, spices, cinnamon sticks and old photo © Karin Hildebrand Lau
Typesetting: MPS Limited
Prepress: Graphic Print Group

ISBN: 978 1 7418 4125 1

Printed and bound in China

Contents

CHAPTER ONE 6-35
Hearty Meals

CHAPTER TWO 36-65
Savoury Pies

CHAPTER THREE 66-89
Soups

CHAPTER FOUR 90-123
Scones, Cookies & Slices

CHAPTER FIVE 124-149
Pastries & Tarts

CHAPTER SIX 150-188
Cakes, Puddings & Muffins

MEASUREMENT TABLE 189

INDEX 190-192

Hearty Meals

A good meal ought to begin with hunger.

French proverb

Traditional Roast Beef with Yorkshire Puddings

Preparation time: 15 minutes
Total cooking time: 1 hour
  45 minutes
Serves 6

2.5 kg (5 lb 8 oz) piece roasting beef
2 garlic cloves, crushed
1 tablespoon plain (all-purpose) flour
2 tablespoons red wine
1¼ cups (315 ml) beef stock

Yorkshire puddings
2 cups (250 g) plain (all-purpose) flour
4 eggs
400 ml (14 fl oz) milk

1 Preheat the oven to 240°C (475°F/Gas 9). Rub the beef with garlic and pepper. Put on a rack in a baking dish, and bake for 15 minutes.

2 To make the puddings, sift the flour and a pinch of salt into a bowl, and make a well in the centre. Add the eggs and whisk. Gradually pour in the milk and whisk to a smooth batter. Pour into a jug, cover and leave for 30 minutes.

3 Reduce the heat to 180°C (350°F/Gas 4), and roast the meat for 50–60 minutes for a rare result, or a little longer for well done. Cover the meat loosely with foil and leave in a warm place for 10–15 minutes. Increase the oven temperature to 220°C (425°F/Gas 7).

4 Pour the pan juices into a jug, then separate the oil from the meat juices, reserving both. Put 1 teaspoon of the oil in each hole of a 12-hole, deep patty pan. Heat in the oven for 2–3 minutes, or until just smoking. Pour in the batter to three-quarters full, put in the oven and bake for 5 minutes. Reduce the oven to 200°C (400°F/Gas 6) and bake for 10 minutes, or until risen and golden.

5 Meanwhile, put the baking dish with the reserved meat juices on the stove over low heat. Add the flour and stir, scraping the bottom of the pan to release any sediment. Cook over medium heat, stirring constantly, until the flour is browned. Combine the wine and stock, and gradually stir into the flour mixture. Cook, stirring constantly, until the gravy boils and thickens. Simmer for 3 minutes.

6 Slice the beef and serve with the gravy, Yorkshire puddings, Brussels sprouts and roast potatoes.

Roast Chicken with Breadcrumb Stuffing

Preparation time: 40 minutes
Total cooking time: 1 hour
  30 minutes
Serves 6

3 rashers back bacon, chopped
6 slices wholegrain bread, crusts
  removed
3 spring (green) onions, chopped
2 tablespoons chopped pecans
2 teaspoons currants
¼ cup (15 g) chopped parsley
1 egg, lightly beaten
¼ cup (60 ml) milk
1.4 kg (3 lb 4 oz) chicken
40 g (1½ oz) butter, melted
1 tablespoon oil
1 tablespoon soy sauce
1 garlic clove, crushed
1½ cups (375 ml) chicken stock
1 tablespoon plain (all-purpose) flour

1 Preheat the oven to 180°C (350°F/Gas 4). Cook the bacon in a dry frying pan over high heat for 5 minutes, or until crisp. Cut the bread into small cubes and place in a bowl. Mix in the bacon, spring (green) onion, pecans, currants, parsley and combined egg and milk. Season with salt and pepper.

2 Remove the giblets and any large amounts of fat from the cavity of the chicken. Pat the chicken dry with paper towels. Spoon the bacon mixture into the chicken cavity. Tuck the wings under the chicken and tie the legs securely with string.

3 Place the chicken on a rack in a deep baking dish. Brush with the combined butter, oil and soy sauce. Pour any remaining mixture into the baking dish with the garlic and half the stock. Roast the chicken for 1–1¼ hours, or until brown and tender, basting occasionally with the pan juices. Pierce between the thigh and body to the bone and check that any juices running out are clear. Put the chicken on a serving dish. Cover loosely with foil and leave in a warm place for 5 minutes before carving.

4 Discard all but 1 tablespoon of the pan juices from the baking dish. Transfer the baking dish to the stove. Add the flour to the pan juices and blend to a smooth paste. Stir constantly over low heat for 5 minutes, or until the mixture browns. Gradually add the remaining stock and stir until the mixture boils and thickens. (Add a little extra stock or water if the gravy is too thick.) Season the gravy with salt and pepper and strain into a jug. Serve the chicken with snow peas (mange tout) and roast potatoes.

Roast Vegetable Mash

Preparation time: 30 minutes
Total cooking time: 1 hour 30 minutes
Serves 4–6

2 large pontiac (desiree) potatoes
400 g (13 oz) pumpkin
400 g (13 oz) orange sweet potato (yam)
2 large parsnips
1 large onion, chopped
2 tomatoes, quartered
6 cloves garlic
2 tablespoons olive oil
30 g (1 oz) butter, chopped

1 Preheat the oven to moderate 180°C (350°F/Gas 4). Peel the potatoes, pumpkin, sweet potato (yam) and parsnips, then cut into large pieces and place in a large baking dish with the onion, tomato and garlic. Drizzle with the oil and sprinkle with salt and freshly ground black pepper.

2 Roast the vegetables for 1½ hours, or until soft and starting to brown, stirring every 30 minutes.

3 Transfer the vegetables to a bowl, add the butter and mash roughly with a fork. Season to taste with salt and freshly ground pepper, and serve.

Roast Potatoes
with Rosemary

Preparation time: 15 minutes
Total cooking time: 30 minutes
Serves 4

750 g (1½ lb) Pink Fir Apple
   potatoes, unpeeled
1½ tablespoons olive oil
8 large cloves garlic, unpeeled
2 tablespoons rosemary leaves

1 Preheat the oven to 200°C (400°F/Gas 6), Cut the potatoes in half lengthways and pat dry. Heat the oil in a large oven dish, add the potatoes and garlic and toss for a minute to coat in the hot oil. Remove from the heat and turn all the potatoes cut-side-up. Sprinkle with rosemary.

2 Bake for 30 minutes, or until cooked and golden. The garlic will be creamy and soft. Serve immediately.

Grandma's Note

Use Kipfler potatoes instead of Pink Fir Apple, if preferred.

Roast Leg of Pork

Preparation time: 30 minutes
Total cooking time: 3 hours 45 minutes
Serves 8

4 kg (9 lb) leg of pork
oil and salt, to rub on pork

Gravy

1 tablespoon brandy or Calvados
2 tablespoons plain (all-purpose) flour
1½ cups (375 ml) chicken stock
½ cup (125 ml) unsweetened apple juice

1 Preheat the oven to 250°C (500°F/Gas 10). Score the rind of the pork with a sharp knife at 3 cm (1 inch) intervals. Rub in some oil and salt to ensure crisp crackling. Place the pork, rind-side-up, on a rack in a large baking dish.

2 Add a little water to the dish. Roast for 30 minutes, or until the rind begins to crackle and bubble. Reduce the heat to 180°C (350°F/Gas 4). Roast for 3 hours 10 minutes. The pork is cooked if the juices run clear when the flesh is pierced with a skewer. Do not cover the pork or the crackling will soften. Leave in a warm place for 10 minutes.

3 To make the gravy, drain off all except 2 tablespoons of the pan juices from the baking dish. Place on top of the stove over medium heat, add the brandy and stir to lift the sediment from the bottom of the pan. Cook for 1 minute. Remove from the heat, stir in the flour and mix well. Return the pan to the heat and cook for 2 minutes, stirring constantly. Gradually add the stock and apple juice, and cook, stirring, until the gravy boils and thickens. Season to taste. Slice the pork and serve with the crackling, gravy, apple sauce, baked apple wedges and vegetables.

Shepherd's Pie

Preparation time: 30 minutes + cooling
Total cooking time: 1 hour 35 minutes
Serves 6

3 tablespoons olive oil
1 large onion, finely chopped
2 cloves garlic, crushed
2 celery sticks, finely chopped
3 carrots, diced
2 bay leaves
1 tablespoon fresh thyme, chopped
1 kg (2 lb) lamb mince
1½ tablespoons plain (all-purpose) flour
½ cup (125 ml) dry red wine
2 tablespoons tomato paste
400 g (13 oz) can crushed tomatoes
1.5 kg (3 lb) potatoes, chopped
¼ cup (60 ml) milk
100 g (3½ oz) butter
½ teaspoon ground nutmeg

1 Heat 2 tablespoons of the oil in a large, heavy-based saucepan and cook the onion for 3–4 minutes, or until softened. Add the garlic, celery, carrot, bay leaves and thyme and cook for 2–3 minutes. Transfer to a bowl and remove the bay leaves.

2 Add the remaining oil to the same pan and cook the mince over high heat for 5–6 minutes, or until it changes colour. Mix in the flour, cook for 1 minute, then pour in the red wine and cook for 2–3 minutes. Return the vegetables to the pan with the tomato paste and crushed tomato. Reduce the heat, cover and simmer for 45 minutes, stirring occasionally. Season and transfer to a shallow 12 cup (3 litre) casserole dish and leave to cool. Preheat the oven to 180°C (350°F/Gas 4).

3 Boil the potatoes in salted water for 20–25 minutes, or until tender. Drain, then mash with the milk and butter until smooth. Season with nutmeg and black pepper. Spoon over the mince and fluff with a fork. Bake for 30 minutes, until golden and crusty.

Toad in the Hole

Preparation time: 3 minutes +
    30 minutes resting
Total cooking time: 30 minutes
Serves 6

110 g (4 oz) plain (all-purpose) flour
2 eggs
150 ml (5 fl oz) milk
4–6 large good-quality sausages
¼ cup (60 ml) oil

1 Sift the flour and a pinch of salt into a large bowl and make a well in the centre. Combine the eggs with the milk and 150 ml (5 fl oz) water and add gradually to the flour, mixing constantly until the batter is smooth and lump free. Cover and leave the batter to rest in the refrigerator for half an hour.

2 Preheat the oven to 220°C (425°F/Gas 7). Fry the sausages in 1 tablespoon of the oil until browned all over but not cooked through. Set aside. Put the rest of the oil in an 18 × 24 cm (7 × 9 inch) ovenproof dish and heat it either on the stove top or in the oven until the oil is smoking hot. The oil must be really hot or the batter will not rise properly.

3 When the oil is hot enough, carefully pour in the batter and add the sausages, spacing them out well so the batter will rise between them. Bake for 20 minutes, or until the batter is well risen and browned. Serve with gravy, steamed beans and grilled tomato.

Sausages and Mash with Onion Gravy

Preparation time: 10 minutes
Total cooking time: 50 minutes
Serves 4

1½ cups (375 ml) beef stock
2 teaspoons cornflour (cornstarch)
2 teaspoons balsamic vinegar
1 tablespoon oil
6 onions, sliced
1.5 kg (3 lb 5 oz) potatoes, chopped
60 g (2¼ oz) butter
½ cup (125 ml) cream
8 beef sausages

1 Mix together 1 tablespoon stock with the cornflour (cornstarch) and stir to dissolve, ensuring there are no lumps. Add to the remaining stock with the vinegar.

2 To make the onion gravy, heat the oil in a large frying pan, add the onion and cook over low heat for 35–40 minutes, or until the onion is soft and beginning to caramelise. Increase the heat and slowly add the stock mixture, stirring constantly until the mixture thickens. Remove from the heat and set aside.

3 Meanwhile, put the potatoes in a large pan of boiling water and cook for 15–20 minutes, or until tender. Drain the potatoes and return them to the pan with the butter and cream. With a potato masher, mash until smooth and creamy. Season to taste with salt and black pepper.

4 Prick the sausages and cook under a hot grill (broiler), turning once, for 10 minutes, or until cooked through.

5 Gently warm the gravy and serve with sausages and mashed potato. Delicious with baked zucchini (courgette).

Bubble and Squeak

Preparation time: 25–30 minutes
Total cooking time: 20 minutes
Serves 4

500 g (1 lb) cold mashed or chopped
 cooked potato
500 g (1 lb) mixture of chopped
 cooked vegetables, such as cabbage,
 carrots, Brussels sprouts, parsnip,
 celery or beans
1 cup (150 g) cooked meat or
 sausage, diced
60 g (2 oz) butter
1 teaspoon white wine vinegar

1 Mix the potato, vegetables and
   meat in a bowl. Heat the butter
   in a heavy-based frying pan, add
   the mixture and cook over
   medium–high heat for 5
   minutes, turning frequently.

2 Flatten and press the mixture in
   the pan and cook for 5–10
   minutes, or until golden and
   crisp on the base. Turn large
   portions of mixture and cook
   for another 5–6 minutes, or
   until the underside is golden.

Sprinkle with vinegar and
season, to taste.

Grandma's Note

Traditionally, day-old, cooked vegetables
are used, with mashed potato and
cabbage forming the base, but mashed
or chopped pumpkin and sweet
potato are also delicious.

Bacon and Onion Rosti Cake

Preparation time: 30 minutes + 1 hour
refrigeration
Total cooking time: 35–40 minutes
Serves 4

850 g (1 lb 12 oz) waxy potatoes, unpeeled
   and halved
60 g (2 oz) butter
6 thin bacon rashers, rind removed,
   chopped
1 small red onion, chopped
1–2 cloves garlic, crushed
2 tablespoons chopped parsley
1 teaspoon each chopped oregano and
   thyme leaves

1 Boil or steam the potato until just
    tender. Drain and refrigerate for 1 hour.
    Peel the potato, grate and put in a bowl.

2 Heat half the butter in a 23 cm (9 inch)
    heavy-based, non-stick pan. Add the
    bacon, onion and garlic and stir for
    2 minutes, or until tender but not
    browned. Add to the potato. Add the
    herbs to the bowl and mix well.

3 Add a little butter to the pan, spread
    the mixture into the pan and press
    with a spatula. Cook for 8 minutes or
    until a crust forms on the base. Shake
    the pan occasionally to stop the
    potato sticking.

4 Slide the rosti onto a greased flat plate,
    add the remaining butter to the pan
    and, when the butter has melted, flip
    the rosti carefully back into the pan on
    its uncooked side. Cook for 6 minutes,
    or until the base is crusty. Serve hot,
    cut into wedges.

Rosemary-Infused Lamb-and-Lentil Casserole

Preparation time: 20 minutes
Total cooking time: 2 hours
*   30 minutes*
Serves 6

1 tablespoon olive oil
1 onion, finely sliced
2 cloves garlic, crushed
1 small carrot, finely chopped
2 teaspoons cumin seeds
½ teaspoon chilli flakes
2 teaspoons finely chopped fresh
    ginger
1 kg (2 lb) boned leg of lamb, cut
    into 4 cm (1½ inch) cubes
2 teaspoons fresh rosemary leaves,
    chopped
3 cups (750 ml) chicken stock
1 cup (185 g) green or brown lentils
3 teaspoons soft brown sugar
2 teaspoons balsamic vinegar

1   Preheat the oven to moderate
    180°C (350°F/Gas 4). Heat half
    the oil in a large, heavy-based
    pan. Add the onion, garlic and
    carrot and cook over medium
    heat for about 5 minutes, or
    until soft and golden. Add the
    cumin seeds, chilli flakes and
    ginger, cook for 1 minute, then
    transfer to a large casserole dish.

2   Heat the remaining oil in the
    pan and brown the lamb in
    batches over high heat. Transfer
    to the casserole dish.

3   Add the rosemary to the pan
    and stir in 2½ cups (625 ml) of
    the stock. Heat until the stock is
    bubbling, then pour into the
    casserole dish. Cover the dish
    and bake in the oven for 1 hour.

4   Add the lentils, sugar and
    vinegar and cook for 1 hour
    more, or until the lentils are
    cooked. If the mixture is too
    thick, stir in the remaining
    stock. Season with salt and
    pepper to taste and serve.

Beef Pot Roast

Preparation time: 15 minutes
Total cooking time: 3 hours
  15 minutes
Serves 6

300 g (10½ oz) pickling onions
2 carrots
3 parsnips, peeled
40 g (1½ oz) butter
1.5 kg (3 lb 5 oz) piece of silverside,
  trimmed of fat
¼ cup (60 ml) dry red wine
1 large tomato, finely chopped
1 cup (250 ml) beef stock

1 Put the onions in a heatproof
bowl and cover with boiling
water. Leave for 1 minute, then
drain well. Allow to cool then
peel off the skins.

2 Cut the carrots and parsnips in
half lengthways then into
even-sized pieces. Heat half the
butter in a large saucepan that will
tightly fit the meat (it will shrink
during cooking), add the onions,
carrot and parsnip and cook,
stirring, over high heat until
browned. Remove from the pan.
Add the remaining butter to the
pan and add the meat, browning
well all over. Increase the heat to
high and pour in the wine. Bring
to the boil, then add the tomato
and stock. Return to the boil,
then reduce the heat to low, cover
and simmer for 2 hours, turning
once. Add the vegetables and
simmer, covered, for 1 hour.

3 Remove the meat from the pan
and put it on a board ready for
carving. Cover with foil and
leave it to stand while finishing
the sauce.

4 Increase the heat to high and
boil the pan juices with the
vegetables for 10 minutes to
reduce and thicken slightly.
Skim off any excess fat, and
season to taste. Slice the meat
and arrange on a serving platter
or individual serving plates with
the vegetables. Drizzle
generously with the pan juices.
Serve with mustard on the side.

Salmon Fishcakes

Preparation time: 1 hour
Total cooking time: 25 minutes
Serves 4

650 g (1 lb 5 oz) floury potatoes,
  peeled
425 g (14 oz) can red salmon,
  drained, bones and skin removed
2 spring (green) onions, finely
  chopped
¼ cup (15 g) chopped fresh parsley
2 teaspoons grated lemon rind
1 egg
5 slices multi-grain bread, crusts
  removed
40 g (1¼ oz) butter
3 tablespoons olive oil

1 Cut the potatoes into chunks
and cook until very tender.
Drain well and mash
until smooth.

2 Place the salmon in a large bowl
and break up the flesh with a
fork. Add the spring (green)
onion, parsley, lemon rind, egg
and mashed potato. Add salt
and pepper, to taste, and stir
well. Shape into rough patties,
using about one third of a cup
for each patty.

3 Chop the bread in a food
processor until fine crumbs
are formed. Gently roll the
patties in the breadcrumbs and
neaten the shape. Press the
breadcrumbs firmly onto the
patties, so they coat well.

4 Place the butter and oil in a large
frying pan. When the butter is
foaming, add the patties and
cook each side for 3–5 minutes
or until golden and browned.
Drain on paper towels. Serve
with lemon wedges.

Cauliflower Cheese

Preparation time: 15 minutes
Total cooking time: 20 minutes
Serves 4

500 g (1 lb 2 oz) cauliflower,
   cut into pieces
30 g (1 oz) butter
30 g (1 oz) plain (all-purpose) flour
1¼ cups (315 ml) warm milk
1 teaspoon Dijon mustard
½ cup (60 g) grated cheddar
   (American) cheese
½ cup (50 g) grated parmesan cheese
2 tablespoons fresh breadcrumbs
3 tablespoons grated cheddar, extra

1 Grease a 1.5 litre (6 cup) heatproof dish. Cook the cauliflower in lightly salted boiling water until just tender. Drain. Put in the dish and keep warm.

2 Melt the butter in a pan. Stir in the flour and cook for 1 minute, or until golden and bubbling. Remove from heat; whisk in the milk and mustard. Return to heat and bring to the boil, stirring constantly. Cook, stirring, over low heat for 2 minutes. Remove from the heat; add the cheeses and stir until melted. Do not reheat the sauce or the oil will come out of the cheese. Season and pour over the cauliflower.

3 Combine the breadcrumbs and extra cheese and sprinkle over the sauce. Grill (broil) until top is browned and bubbling. Serve immediately.

Rustic Hotpot

Preparation time: 40 minutes +
   1 hour refrigeration
Total cooking time: 2 hours
Serves 4

2 tablespoons olive oil
8 lamb shanks
2 onions, sliced
4 cloves garlic, finely chopped
3 bay leaves, torn in half
1–2 teaspoons hot paprika
2 teaspoons sweet paprika
1 tablespoon plain (all-purpose) flour
3 tablespoons tomato paste
6 cups (1.5 litres) vegetable stock
4 potatoes, chopped
4 carrots, sliced
3 sticks celery, thickly sliced
3 tomatoes, seeded and chopped

1 To make the lamb stock, heat
   1 tablespoon of the oil in a large,
   heavy-based pan over medium
   heat. Brown the shanks well
   in two batches and drain on
   paper towels.

2 Add the remaining tablespoon of
   oil to the pan and cook the
   onion, garlic and bay leaves over
   low heat for 10 minutes, stirring
   regularly. Add the paprikas and
   flour and cook, stirring
   continuously, for 2 minutes.
   Gradually add the combined
   tomato paste and stock. Bring to
   the boil, stirring continuously,
   and return the shanks to the pan.
   Reduce the heat to low and
   simmer, covered, for 1½ hours,
   stirring occasionally.

3 Remove the bay leaves and
   discard. Remove the shanks,
   allow to cool slightly and then
   cut the meat from the bone.
   Discard the bones. Cut the meat
   into pieces and refrigerate.
   Refrigerate the stock for about
   1 hour, or until fat forms on the
   surface and can be spooned off.

4 Return the meat to the soup
   along with the potato, carrot and
   celery and bring to the boil.
   Reduce the heat and simmer for
   15 minutes. Season and add the
   chopped tomato to serve.

Fisherman's Pie

Preparation time: 40 minutes
Total cooking time: 1 hour
Serves 4

800 g (1 lb 10 oz) white fish fillets
1½ cups (375 ml) milk
1 onion, roughly chopped
2 cloves
50 g (1¾ oz) butter
2 tablespoons plain (all-purpose) flour
pinch of ground nutmeg
2 tablespoons chopped fresh parsley
1 cup (150 g) peas
750 g (1½ lb) potatoes, quartered
2 tablespoons hot milk
3 tablespoons grated cheddar
   (American) cheese

1 Place the fish in a pan and cover
   with the milk. Add the onion and
cloves and bring to the boil.
Reduce the heat and simmer for 5
minutes, or until the fish is cooked
and flakes easily with a fork.

2 Preheat the oven to 180°C
   (350°F/Gas 4). Remove the fish
   from the pan, reserving the milk
   and onion. Discard the cloves.
   Allow the fish to cool then
   remove any bones and flake into
   bite-sized pieces with a fork.

3 Heat half of the butter in a pan,
   stir in the flour and cook, stirring,
   for 1 minute. Slowly add the
   reserved milk, stirring constantly
   until smooth. Cook, stirring,
   until the sauce begins to bubble,
   then cook for another minute.

Remove from the heat, cool
slightly, then add the nutmeg,
parsley and peas. Season and
gently fold in the fish. Spoon into
a 1.25 litre (42 fl oz) casserole dish.

4 Cook the potatoes in boiling
   water until tender. Drain and add
   the hot milk and remaining
   butter. Mash until very smooth.
   Add the cheese. If the mash is
   very stiff you can add a little more
   milk, but it should be fairly firm.

5 Spoon the potato over the filling
   and rough up with a fork. For a
   neater topping, spoon the potato
   into a piping bag and pipe over
   the filling. Bake for 30 minutes
   to heat through.

Meatballs in Tomato Sauce

Preparation time: 40 minutes
Total cooking time: 1 hour
* 40 minutes*
Serves 6

500 g (1 lb) lean veal mince
1 onion, very finely chopped
4 cloves garlic, finely chopped
1 egg white, lightly beaten
1 cup (80 g) fresh white
  breadcrumbs
½ cup (30 g) finely chopped fresh
  parsley
3 tablespoons finely chopped fresh
  oregano
cooking oil spray
1.5 kg (3 lb) ripe tomatoes
2 onions, finely sliced
½ cup (125 g) tomato paste
½ teaspoon sugar
350 g (11 oz) penne pasta

1 Combine the veal mince, onion, half the garlic, the egg white, breadcrumbs, two-thirds of the parsley and 1 tablespoon of the oregano in a large bowl. Season and mix well with your hands. Shape into 36 small balls. Spray a large non-stick frying pan with oil. Cook a third of the meatballs over high heat for 4–5 minutes, or until browned, turning constantly to prevent the meatballs sticking. Remove from the pan and repeat with the remaining meatballs.

2 Score a cross in the base of each tomato, place in a heatproof bowl and cover with boiling water. Leave for 1 minute, or until the skins start to come away. Drain, plunge into a bowl of iced water, then peel away the skin and roughly chop the flesh.

3 Lightly spray the base of a large, deep non-stick saucepan. Add the sliced onion and remaining garlic and cook over low heat for 2–3 minutes, stirring constantly. Add 2 tablespoons water, cover and cook gently for 5 minutes to soften the onion. Stir in the tomato and tomato paste. Cover and simmer for 10 minutes, uncover and simmer gently for 40 minutes. Add the meatballs, cover and simmer for another 15–20 minutes, or until the meatballs are just cooked. Add the sugar, remaining parsley and oregano and season well.

4 Cook the penne in a large pan of boiling salted water until al dente, then drain. Serve with the meatballs.

Lamb's Liver and Bacon

Preparation time: 10 minutes
Total cooking time: 10 minutes
Serves 4

500 g (1 lb 2 oz) lamb's liver
1 tablespoon olive oil
1 large onion, sliced
125 g (4½ oz) streaky bacon, cut
 into strips
30 g (1 oz) butter
1 tablespoon plain (all-purpose) flour
300 ml (10 fl oz) beef stock
2 tablespoons chopped parsley

1 Remove the membrane and tubes from the liver and slice horizontally into thin slices.

2 Heat the oil in a large non-stick frying pan and cook the onion and bacon until browned. Remove from the pan and keep warm.

3 Turn up the heat and add the butter to the frying pan until it sizzles. Quickly cook the liver in batches over high heat for about 1 minute on each side. Do not overcook the liver or it will become tough. Return all the liver to the pan with the bacon and onion. Sprinkle the flour over the top and toss to coat. Gradually add the stock and stir until the sauce boils and thickens. Season to taste. Stir in the parsley and serve immediately with fried tomato slices and mashed potato.

Chicken and Mushroom Casserole

Preparation time: 20 minutes
Total cooking time: 1 hour
Serves 4

20 g (1 oz) dried porcini mushrooms
¼ cup (30 g) plain (all-purpose) flour
1.5 kg (3 lb 5 oz) chicken pieces
2 tablespoons oil
1 large onion, chopped
2 garlic cloves, crushed
¼ cup (60 ml) chicken stock
⅓ cup (80 ml) white wine
425 g (15 oz) can tomatoes
1 tablespoon balsamic vinegar
3 thyme sprigs
1 bay leaf
300 g (10½ oz) field mushrooms,
   thickly sliced

1 Preheat the oven to 180°C (350°F/Gas 4). Put the porcini mushrooms in a bowl and cover with 60 ml (¼ cup) boiling water. Leave to rehydrate for 5 minutes.

2 Season the flour with salt and pepper. Lightly toss the chicken in flour to coat. Shake off any excess.

3 Heat the oil in a casserole dish, and cook the chicken in batches until well browned. Set aside. Add the onion and garlic to the casserole dish and cook until the onion softens. Stir in the chicken stock.

4 Put the chicken in the casserole dish with the porcini mushrooms (and any remaining liquid), wine, tomatoes, vinegar, thyme and bay leaf. Cover and cook in the oven for 30 minutes.

5 After 30 minutes, add the field mushrooms. Return to the oven and cook, uncovered, for a further 15–20 minutes, or until the sauce thickens slightly. Serve immediately.

Cottage Pie

Preparation time: 30 minutes
Total cooking time: 1 hour
  30 minutes
Serves 6–8

2 tablespoons olive oil
2 onions, chopped
2 carrots, diced
1 celery stick, diced
1 kg (2 lb) beef mince
2 tablespoons plain
  (all-purpose) flour
1½ cups (375 ml) beef stock
1 tablespoon soy sauce
1 tablespoon Worcestershire sauce
2 tablespoons tomato sauce
1 tablespoon tomato paste
2 bay leaves
2 teaspoons chopped fresh
  flat-leaf parsley

Topping

800 g (1 lb 10 oz) potatoes, diced
400 g (13 oz) parsnips, diced
30 g (1 oz) butter
½ cup (125 ml) milk

1 Heat the oil in a large frying pan over medium heat and cook the onion, carrot and celery, stirring occasionally, for 5 minutes, or until softened and lightly coloured. Add the mince and cook for 7 minutes, then stir in the flour and cook for 2 minutes. Add the stock, soy sauce, Worcestershire sauce, tomato sauce, tomato paste and bay leaves and simmer over low heat for 30 minutes, stirring occasionally. Leave to cool. Remove the bay leaves and stir in the parsley.

2 To make the topping, boil the potato and parsnip in salted water for 15–20 minutes, or until cooked through. Drain, return to the pan and mash with the butter and enough of the milk to make a firm mash.

3 Preheat the oven to 180°C (350°F/Gas 4) and lightly grease a 10 cup (2.5 litre) ovenproof dish. Spoon the filling into the dish and spread the topping over it. Fluff with a fork. Bake for 25 minutes, or until golden.

Beef Casserole with Caraway Dumplings

Preparation time: 1 hour
Total cooking time: 1 hour
*   15 minutes*
Serves 6

1.5 kg (3 lb) round or topside steak,
    trimmed and cut into 3 cm
    (1¼ inch) cubes
½ cup (60 g) plain (all-purpose) flour
¼ teaspoon ground black pepper
⅓ cup (80 ml) olive oil
1 clove garlic, crushed
2 onions, sliced
1 teaspoon ground sweet paprika
½ teaspoon ground cinnamon
⅓ cup (80 ml) red wine
½ cup (125 ml) beef stock
½ teaspoon dried mixed herbs
⅔ cup (160 g) tomato pasta sauce
3 large red capsicums (peppers)

Dumplings
1½ cups (185 g) self-raising flour
65 g (2¼ oz) butter
½ cup (125 ml) milk
1 teaspoon caraway seeds
1 tablespoon milk, extra

1 Preheat the oven to moderate 180°C
(350°F/Gas 4). Toss the meat lightly in
the combined flour and pepper, and
shake off any excess.

2 Heat 2 tablespoons of the oil in a
heavy-based saucepan. Cook the meat
quickly in small batches over medium–
high heat until well browned. Drain
on paper towels.

3 Heat the remaining oil in the pan.
Cook the garlic and onion over
medium heat, stirring, for 2 minutes,
or until soft.

4 Return the meat to the pan with the
spices, wine, stock, mixed herbs and
tomato pasta sauce. Bring to the boil,
then remove from the heat and transfer
to a deep casserole dish. Bake, covered,
for 45 minutes. Remove from the oven
and remove the lid. Increase the oven
to very hot 240°C (475°F/Gas 9).

5 Halve the capsicums (peppers)
lengthways and remove the seeds.
Grill, skin-side up, under a hot grill for
10 minutes, or until the skin blackens
and blisters. Remove from the grill and
allow to cool. Carefully peel off the
skins. Cut the capsicum into 2 cm
(¾ inch) wide strips. Arrange the
roasted capsicum over the meat.

6 To make the dumplings, process the
flour and butter in a food processor for
10 seconds, or until fine and crumbly.
Add the milk all at once and process
for 10 seconds, or until a soft dough is
formed. Turn the dough onto a lightly
floured surface. Add the caraway seeds
and knead for 1 minute, or until
smooth. Press the dough out to a 1 cm
(½ inch) round. Cut 4 cm (1½ inch)
rounds using a fluted cutter. Top the
casserole with the dumplings and
brush with the extra milk. Return the
casserole to the oven, uncovered, for
15 minutes, or until the dumplings are
puffed and golden.

Lancashire Hotpot

Preparation time: 20 minutes
Total cooking time: 2 hours
Serves 8

8 lamb forequarter chops
4 lamb kidneys
¼ cup (30 g) plain (all-purpose) flour
50 g (1¾ oz) butter
4 potatoes, thinly sliced
2 large onions, sliced
1 large carrot, chopped
1¾ cups (440 ml) beef stock
2 teaspoons chopped thyme
1 bay leaf
melted butter, extra

1 Preheat the oven to 160°C (315°F/Gas 2–3), and brush a large casserole dish with melted butter or oil. Trim the chops of excess fat and sinew, then remove the cores from the kidneys and cut into quarters. Toss the chops and kidneys in flour, shaking off and reserving the excess. Heat the butter in a frying pan and brown the chops quickly on both sides. Remove the chops from the pan and brown the kidneys.

2 Layer half the potato slices in the base of the casserole and top with the chops and kidneys.

3 Add the onion and carrot to the pan and cook until the carrot begins to brown. Layer on top of the chops and kidneys.

Sprinkle the reserved flour over the base of the pan and fry, stirring, until dark brown. Gradually pour in the stock and bring to the boil, stirring. Season well and add the thyme and bay leaf. Reduce the heat and simmer for 10 minutes. Pour into the casserole.

4 Layer the remaining potato over the meat and vegetables. Cover and cook in the oven for 1¼ hours. Increase the temperature to 180°C (350°F/Gas 4), brush the potato with the extra butter and cook, uncovered, for 20 minutes, or until the potato is brown.

Meat Loaf

Preparation time: 25 minutes
Total cooking time: 1 hour
    15 minutes
Serves 6

125 g (4½ oz) streaky bacon,
    trimmed and chopped
500 g (1 lb 2 oz) minced
    (ground) beef
500 g (1 lb 2 oz) minced
    (ground) pork
1 onion, coarsely grated
2 garlic cloves, crushed
2 cups (160 g) fresh breadcrumbs
2 teaspoons thyme leaves
1 egg, lightly beaten
1 tablespoon red wine vinegar
2 teaspoons soft brown sugar

1 Preheat the oven to 180°C
   (350°F/Gas 4). Lightly grease a
   loaf tin then line with a single
   sheet of baking paper, leaving
   the paper to overhang on the
   long sides of the tin.

2 Heat a non-stick frying pan,
   add the bacon, and cook,
   stirring, until crispy. Drain
   on paper towels.

3 Place the meat, onion, garlic,
   breadcrumbs, thyme, egg, vinegar,
   sugar and bacon in a large bowl.
   Season and mix together using
   your hands. Don't overmix or the
   meat loaf will become too dense
   when it is cooked.

4 Spoon the mixture into the tin
   and press down gently. Smooth
   the top and bake for 1 hour
   10 minutes, or until browned
   and cooked through. Test if it is
   cooked by pushing a metal
skewer or sharp knife into the
centre, leaving it for 3 seconds,
and then pulling it out and
holding it against your wrist. If it
is really hot, it is cooked through;
if not, cook a little longer. Leave
for 5 minutes and pour the
cooking juices into a jug. Lift out
the meat loaf using the
overhanging baking paper. Cut
into slices with a serrated knife
and drizzle with the cooking
juices. Serve with tomato sauce,
peas, corn and potatoes.

Corned Beef

Preparation time: 5 minutes
Total cooking time: 1 hour
*   40 minutes*
Serves 6–8

1 tablespoon oil
1.5 kg (3 lb) piece corned silverside,
    trimmed
1 tablespoon white vinegar
1 tablespoon soft brown sugar
4 cloves
4 black peppercorns
2 bay leaves
1 clove garlic, crushed
1 large sprig fresh parsley
4 carrots
4 potatoes
6 small onions

Onion sauce
30 g (1 oz) butter
2 white onions, chopped
2 tablespoons plain (all-purpose) flour
1⅓ cups (330 ml) milk

Horseradish cream
¼ cup (60 ml) horseradish relish
1 tablespoon white vinegar
½ cup (125 ml) cream, whipped

1 Heat the oil in a deep, heavy-
   based saucepan. Cook the meat
   over medium–high heat, turning
   until well browned all over.
   Remove the pan from the heat
   and add the vinegar, sugar,
   cloves, peppercorns, bay leaves,
   garlic and parsley.

2 Pour over enough water to
   cover. Cover and return to the
   heat, reduce the heat and bring
   slowly to simmering point.
   Simmer for 30 minutes.

3 Cut the carrots and potatoes
   into large pieces and add to the
   pan with the onions. Simmer,
   covered, for 1 hour, or until
   tender. Remove the vegetables
   and keep warm. Reserve ½ cup
   (125 ml) of the cooking liquid.

4 To make the onion sauce, heat
   the butter in a small saucepan.
   Cook the onion gently for
   10 minutes, or until soft but not
   browned. Transfer the onion to
   a bowl. Add the flour to the pan
   and stir over low heat for
   2 minutes, or until the flour is
   lightly golden. Gradually add
   the milk and the reserved

cooking liquid, and stir until the
sauce boils and thickens. Boil
for 1 minute, then remove from
the heat and stir in the onion.
Season to taste.

5 To make the horseradish cream,
   combine all of the ingredients in
   a bowl until smooth.

6 Drain the meat from the pan,
   discarding the remaining liquid
   and spices. Slice the meat, and
   serve it with the vegetables, onion
   sauce and horseradish cream.

Steak and Kidney Pudding

Preparation time: 25 minutes
Total cooking time: 5 hours
Serves 4

2¾ cups (340 g) self-raising flour
150 g (5½ oz) butter, frozen and
  grated
700 g (1 lb 9 oz) chuck steak, cubed
200 g (7 oz) ox kidney, cubed
1 small onion, finely chopped
2 teaspoons chopped parsley
1 tablespoon plain (all-purpose) flour
1 teaspoon Worcestershire sauce
¾ cup (185 ml) beef stock

1 Grease a 6 cup (1.5 litre)
pudding basin with melted
butter, and put a round of
baking paper in the bottom.
Place the empty basin in a large
pan on a trivet or upturned
saucer and pour in enough cold
water to come halfway up the
side of the basin. Remove the
basin and put the water on
to boil.

2 Sift the flour into a bowl and
add the butter and a pinch of
salt. Mix together with a
flat-bladed knife and add
enough water to form a soft
dough. Reserve one third of the
dough and roll the rest out to a
circle about 1 cm (¼ inch)
thick. Sprinkle with flour and
fold it in half. Using a rolling
pin, roll the straight edge away
from you, making sure the two
halves don't stick together, to
form a bag shape. Fit the bag
into the pudding basin, leaving
a little hanging over the edge.
Brush out any excess flour.

3 Mix the steak, kidney, onion,
parsley and flour together in a
bowl. Season and add the
Worcestershire sauce. Put the
mixture into the pastry case and
add enough stock to come
three-quarters of the way up the
meat. Roll out the remaining
pastry to form a lid. Fold the
overhanging pastry into the
bowl and dampen the edge with
water. Put the lid on and press
the edges together.

4 Lay a sheet of foil then a sheet of
baking paper on the work surface,
and make a large pleat in the
middle. Grease with melted
butter. Place paper-side-down
across the top of the basin and tie
string securely around the rim and
over the top of the basin to make
a handle for lifting the pudding.

5 Lower the basin into the
simmering water and cover with a
tight-fitting lid. Cook for 5 hours,
checking every hour and topping
up with boiling water as needed.
Serve from the basin.

Savoury Pies

There is no love sincerer than the love of food.

George Bernard Shaw

Rosemary Lamb Cobbler

Preparation time: 30 minutes
Total cooking time: 2 hours
Serves 4–6

600 g (1¼ lb) boned lamb leg, cut into
   small chunks
¼ cup (30 g) plain (all-purpose)
   flour, seasoned
30 g (1 oz) butter
2 tablespoons olive oil
8 spring (green) onions, chopped
3 cloves garlic, crushed
2 cups (500 ml) beef stock
1 cup (250 ml) dry white wine
2 teaspoons wholegrain mustard
2 teaspoons finely chopped fresh rosemary
2 celery sticks, sliced
1 teaspoon grated lemon rind
1 teaspoon lemon juice
½ cup (125 g) sour cream

Cobbler topping
¾ cup (185 ml) milk
1 egg
2 tablespoons melted butter
1½ cups (185 g) plain (all-purpose) flour
2 teaspoons baking powder
1 teaspoon finely chopped fresh rosemary
2 tablespoons finely chopped fresh
   flat-leaf parsley

1 Put the lamb pieces and flour in a plastic
bag and shake well to evenly coat the
lamb. Shake off any excess.

2 Heat the butter and 1 tablespoon of the
olive oil in a large saucepan over high heat,
then cook half the lamb for 5 minutes, or
until well browned. Add the remaining oil
if needed and cook the remaining lamb.

3 Add half the spring (green) onion to
the pan with the garlic and cook for
30 seconds, or until the onion is
softened. Return all the lamb to the pan
with the stock, wine, mustard, rosemary,
celery, lemon rind and juice and bring
to the boil. Reduce the heat and simmer,
stirring occasionally, for 1¼ hours, or
until the lamb is tender and the sauce
has thickened.

4 Remove from the heat and stir a little of
the sauce into the sour cream, then stir
it all back into the lamb mixture with
the remaining spring onion. Leave to
cool while you make the topping.

5 Preheat the oven to 190°C (375°F/Gas 5).
To make the topping, combine the milk,
egg and melted butter in a large bowl.
Add the combined sifted flour and
baking powder with the herbs, 1 teaspoon
salt and some cracked black pepper
and stir until you have a thick, sticky
batter – you may need to add a little
more flour if it is too wet, or milk if it
is too dry.

6 Spoon the lamb into a deep 18 cm
(7 inch) pie dish and, using two spoons,
cover the top with small dollops of the
batter, leaving a little space for spreading.
Cook for 30 minutes, or until the topping
is risen and golden.

Game Pie

Preparation time: 50 minutes +
   overnight setting
Total cooking time: 5 hours
Serves 4–6

Jelly
any bones reserved from the game meat
2 pig's trotters
1 onion, quartered
1 carrot, roughly chopped
1 celery stick, chopped
2 bay leaves
6 black peppercorns

Filling
250 g (8 oz) pork belly, finely diced
4 rashers streaky bacon, chopped
400 g (13 oz) game meat (e.g. rabbit,
   pheasant), removed from carcass
   and finely diced (bones reserved)
½ small onion, finely chopped
½ teaspoon ground nutmeg
½ teaspoon ground cinnamon
2 dried juniper berries, crushed
1 teaspoon chopped fresh thyme

Pastry
4 cups (500 g) plain (all-purpose) flour
90 g (3 oz) lard
1 egg, lightly beaten, to glaze

1 To make the stock for the jelly,
   place all the ingredients and
   7 cups (1.75 litres) water in a
   large saucepan and bring to the
   boil over high heat. Remove any
   froth that forms on the surface.
   Reduce the heat and simmer for
   3 hours, skimming off any froth
   occasionally. Strain, return to
   the pan and cook uncovered
   until the liquid has reduced to
   about 2 cups (500 ml). Cool,
   then refrigerate.

2 To make the filling, combine
   all the ingredients in a bowl.
   Season well.

3 To make the pastry, sift the flour
   and ½ teaspoon salt into a large
   bowl and make a well in the
   centre. Bring 200 ml (6½ fl oz)
   water and the lard to the boil in
   a saucepan. Pour the boiling
   liquid into the flour and mix
   with a wooden spoon to form a
   dough. Gather together and lift
   onto a lightly floured work
   surface. Press together until
   smooth. Keep the dough warm
   by covering with foil and
   putting it in a warm place.

4 Preheat the oven to 190°C
   (375°F/Gas 5). Grease an 18 cm
   (7 inch) springform tin. While
   the pastry is still warm, roll out
   two-thirds of the dough between
   two sheets of baking paper and
   line the base and side of the tin,
   leaving some overhanging. Spoon
   the filling into the tin, pressing
   down well. Roll out the remaining
   dough to about 4 mm (¼ inch)
   thick and 20 cm (8 inches) across.
   Place on top of the tin and pinch
   the edges together to seal. Trim the
   edges and cut a small hole in the
   top of the pie.

5 Roll out the pastry trimmings to
   make decorations, securing to
   the pie top with a little beaten
   egg. Glaze the top of the pie
   with egg and bake for 1 hour
   20 minutes. Cover the top with
   foil after about 45 minutes to
   prevent it colouring too much.

6 Remove the pie from the oven
   and allow to cool for about
   25 minutes. Gently remove from
   the tin, brush the top and sides
   with beaten egg and place on a
   baking tray (sheet). Return to the
   oven and cook for another
   20 minutes until golden brown
   and firm to touch. Remove from
   the oven and cool.

7 Warm the jelly to a pouring
   consistency. Place a small piping
   nozzle into the hole in the pie and
   pour in a little of the jelly. Leave to
   settle, then pour in more jelly
   until the pie is full. Fill the pie
   completely so there are no
   gaps when the jelly sets.
   Refrigerate overnight but
   serve at room temperature.

Cheese and Onion Pie

Preparation time: 25 minutes +
10 minutes cooling
Total cooking time: 45 minutes
Serves 4

2 tablespoons olive oil
2 onions, chopped
1½ cups (185 g) grated cheddar
   (American) cheese
1 tablespoon chopped fresh
   flat-leaf parsley
1 teaspoon English mustard
2 teaspoons Worcestershire sauce
2 eggs, beaten
2 sheets puff pastry

1 Preheat the oven to 190°C
   (375°F/Gas 5). Heat the oil in a
   large frying pan over medium
   heat, add the onion and cook for
   5–7 minutes, or until soft and
   golden. Transfer to a bowl and
   allow to cool for 10 minutes.

2 Add the cheese, parsley, mustard
   and Worcestershire sauce to the
   onion and mix well. Add half the
   egg to the bowl and season well.

3 Cut each sheet of pastry into a
   23 cm (9 inch) circle. Lay one
   sheet of pastry on a lined baking
   tray (sheet). Spread the filling

over the pastry base, piling it
higher in the middle and leaving
a narrow border. Lightly brush
the border with some of the
beaten egg and place the second
sheet on top, stretching it slightly
to neatly fit the bottom. Press
and seal the edges well and brush
the top with the remaining
beaten egg. Cut two slits in the
top for steam to escape.

4 Bake for 10 minutes, then
   reduce the heat to 180°C
   (350°F/Gas 4) and cook for
   another 20–25 minutes, or until
   the pastry is crisp and golden.

Ham and Chicken Pie

Preparation time: 40 minutes
Total cooking time: 1 hour
Serves 6–8

3 cups (375 g) plain
   (all-purpose) flour
180 g (6 oz) butter, chilled and cubed
2–3 tablespoons iced water
1 egg, lightly beaten, to glaze

Filling
1 kg (2 lb) chicken mince
1 teaspoon dried mixed herbs
2 eggs, lightly beaten
3 spring (green) onions,
   finely chopped
2 tablespoons chopped fresh parsley
2 teaspoons French mustard
⅓ cup (80 ml) cream
200 g (6½ oz) sliced leg ham

1 Preheat the oven to 180°C (350°F/Gas 4). Mix the flour and butter in a food processor for 20 seconds or until fine and crumbly. Add the water and process for 20 seconds or until the mixture comes together. Turn onto a lightly floured surface and press together until smooth. Roll out two-thirds of the pastry to line a 20 cm (8 inch) springform tin, leaving some pastry overhanging the side. Cover with plastic wrap and refrigerate until required. Wrap the remaining pastry in plastic wrap and refrigerate.

2 To make the filling, mix together the chicken, herbs, eggs, onions, parsley, mustard and cream and season well.

3 Spoon a third of the filling into the pastry-lined tin and smooth the surface. Top with half the ham and then another chicken layer followed by the remaining ham and then a final layer of chicken filling.

4 Brush around the inside edge of pastry with egg. Roll out the remaining pastry to make a pie top, pressing the pastry edges together. Trim the edge. Decorate the top with pastry trimmings. Brush the pie top with beaten egg and bake for 1 hour or until golden brown.

Chicken and Leek Pie

Preparation time: 20 minutes
Total cooking time: 40 minutes
Serves 4

60 g (2 oz) butter
2 large leeks, finely sliced
4 spring (green) onions, sliced
1 clove garlic, crushed
¼ cup (30 g) plain (all-purpose) flour
1½ cups (375 ml) chicken stock
½ cup (125 ml) cream
1 barbecued chicken, chopped
2 sheets puff pastry
¼ cup (60 ml) milk

1 Preheat the oven to 200°C (400°F/ Gas 6). In a pan, melt the butter and add the leek, onion and garlic. Cook over low heat for 6 minutes, or until the leek is soft but not browned. Sprinkle in the flour and mix well. Pour in the stock gradually and cook, stirring well, until thick and smooth. Stir in the cream and add the chicken.

2 Put the mixture in a shallow 20 cm (8 inch) pie dish and set aside to cool.

3 Cut a circle out of one of the sheets of pastry to cover the top of the pie. Paint around the rim of the pie dish with a little milk. Put the pastry on top and seal around the edge firmly. Trim off any overhanging pastry and decorate the edge with a fork.

4 Cut the other sheet of pastry into 1 cm (½ inch) strips and roll each strip up loosely like a snail. Arrange the spirals on top of the pie, starting from the middle and leaving gaps between them. The spirals may not cover the whole surface of the pie. Make a few small holes between the spirals to let out any steam and brush the top of the pie lightly with milk. Bake for 25–30 minutes, or until the top is brown and crispy. Make sure the spirals look well cooked and are not raw in the middle.

Beef and Caramelised Onion Pie

Preparation time: 40 minutes +
  20 minutes cooling
Total cooking time: 2 hours
  20 minutes
Serves 6–8

⅓ cup (80 ml) oil
2 large red onions, thinly sliced
1 teaspoon dark brown sugar
1 kg (2 lb) lean rump steak, diced
¼ cup (30 g) plain (all-purpose)
  flour, seasoned
2 cloves garlic, crushed
225 g (7 oz) button
  mushrooms, sliced
1 cup (250 ml) beef stock
150 ml (5 fl oz) stout
1 tablespoon tomato paste
1 tablespoon Worcestershire sauce
1 tablespoon chopped fresh thyme
350 g (11 oz) potatoes, diced
2 carrots, diced
600 g (1¼ lb) quick flaky pastry
1 egg, lightly beaten

1   Heat 2 tablespoons of the oil in
    a frying pan over medium heat
    and cook the onion for
    5 minutes, or until light brown,
    then add the sugar and cook for
    7–8 minutes, or until the onion
    caramelises. Remove from the
    pan. Wipe the pan clean.

2   Toss the beef in flour and shake
    off the excess. Heat the
    remaining oil in the same pan
    and cook the meat in batches
    over high heat until browned.
    Return all the meat to the pan,
    add the garlic and mushrooms

and cook for 2 minutes. Add the
stock, stout, tomato paste,
Worcestershire sauce and thyme.
Bring to the boil, then reduce
the heat and simmer, covered, for
1 hour. Add the potato and carrot
and simmer for 30 minutes.
Remove from the heat and allow
to cool.

3   Preheat the oven to 190°C
    (375°F/Gas 5). Grease a 5 cup
    (1.25 litre) pie dish. Pour in the
    filling, then top with the onion.
    Roll the pastry out between two
    sheets of baking paper until it is

2.5 cm (1 inch) wider than the
pie dish. Cut a 2 cm (¾ inch)
strip around the edge of the
pastry circle, brush with water
and place damp-side-down on
the rim of the dish.

4   Cover with the remaining
    pastry, pressing the edges
    together. Knock up the rim by
    making small slashes in the
    edges of the pastry with the back
    of a knife. Re-roll the trimmings
    and use them to decorate the
    pie. Brush with egg and bake for
    25 minutes, or until golden.

Vegetable Lattice Pie

*Preparation time: 40 minutes +
chilling*
Total cooking time: 1 hour
Serves 6

185 g (6 oz) butter
2 cups (250 g) plain (all-purpose) flour
3 tablespoons iced water

Filling

1 tablespoon oil
1 onion, finely chopped
1 small red capsicum
    (pepper), chopped
1 small green capsicum
    (pepper), chopped
150 g (5 oz) pumpkin, chopped
1 small potato, chopped
100 g (3½ oz) broccoli, cut into
    small florets
1 carrot, chopped
3 tablespoons plain (all-purpose) flour
1 cup (250 ml) milk
2 egg yolks
½ cup (60 g) grated cheddar
    (American) cheese
1 egg, lightly beaten, to glaze

1 Chop 125 g (4 oz) of the butter.
Sift the flour into a large bowl
and add the chopped butter.
Using your fingertips, rub the
butter into the flour until the
mixture is fine and crumbly. Add
almost all the water and use a
knife to mix to a firm dough,
adding more water if necessary.
Turn onto a lightly floured
surface and press together until
smooth. Divide the dough in
half, roll out one portion and line
a deep 20 cm (8 inch) fluted flan
tin. Refrigerate for 20 minutes.
Roll the remaining pastry out to
a 25 cm (10 inch) diameter

circle. Cut into strips and lay
half of them on a sheet of
baking paper, leaving a 2 cm
(¾ inch) gap between each strip.
Interweave the remaining strips
to form a lattice pattern. Cover
with plastic wrap and refrigerate,
keeping flat, until firm.

2 Preheat the oven to 180°C
(350°F/Gas 4). Cut a sheet of
greaseproof paper to cover the
pastry-lined tin. Spread a layer
of baking beads or dried beans
or rice over the paper. Bake for
10 minutes, remove from the
oven and discard the paper
and beans. Bake for another
10 minutes or until golden.
Remove and allow to cool.

3 Heat the oil in a frying pan.
Add the onion and cook for
2 minutes or until soft. Add the
caspicum (pepper) and cook,
stirring, for another 3 minutes.

Steam or boil the remaining
vegetables until just tender;
drain and cool. Combine the
onion, capsicum and the other
vegetables in a large bowl.

4 Heat the remaining butter in a
small pan. Add the flour and
cook, stirring, for 2 minutes. Add
the milk gradually, stirring until
smooth after each addition. Stir
until the sauce boils and thickens.
Boil for 1 minute and then
remove from the heat. Add the
egg yolks and cheese and stir until
smooth. Pour over the vegetables
and stir together. Pour into the
pastry case and brush the edges
with egg. Using the baking paper
to help, invert the lattice over the
vegetables, trim the edges and
brush with a little egg. Press the
edges lightly to seal to the cooked
pastry. Brush the top with egg
and bake for 30 minutes or until
the pastry is golden.

Lamb Shank Pie

*Preparation time: 30 minutes +
   2 hours chilling*
*Total cooking time: 3 hours
   10 minutes*
Serves 6

8 lamb shanks
½ cup (60 g) plain (all-purpose) flour
2 tablespoons olive oil
4 red onions, quartered
8 cloves garlic, peeled
1 cup (250 ml) red wine
1 litre beef stock
2 tablespoons finely chopped fresh
   rosemary
6 whole black peppercorns
¼ cup (30 g) cornflour (cornstarch)
375 g (12 oz) puff pastry
1 egg, lightly beaten

1 Preheat the oven to 220°C
   (425°F/Gas 7). Lightly dust the
   shanks with flour, shaking off
   the excess. Heat the oil in a large
   frying pan and cook the shanks
   for 2 minutes each side, or until
   well browned. Transfer to a deep
   roasting tin and add the onion,
   garlic, wine, stock, rosemary and
   peppercorns. Cover and bake for
   1 hour.

2 Stir the mixture, uncover and
   return to the oven for 1 hour
   10 minutes, stirring occasionally,
   until the meat falls off the bones.

3 Remove the lamb bones with
   tongs. Mix the cornflour
   (cornstarch) with 2 tablespoons
   water, then stir into the tin.
   Return to the oven for
   10 minutes, or until thickened.
   Transfer to a large bowl, cool,
   then refrigerate for at least
   2 hours, or overnight.

4 Preheat the oven to moderate
   180°C (350°F/Gas 4). Grease a
   23 cm (9 inch) pie plate with a
   rim. Spoon in the filling. Roll
   the pastry out between two
   sheets of baking paper until a
   little wider than the plate. Cut a
   2 cm (¾ inch) strip around the
   edge of the pastry, brush with
   water and place damp-side-
   down on the rim. Cover with
   the pastry circle, pressing down
   on the edges. Use the back of a
   knife to make small slashes
   around the edge. Trim, then
   re-roll the scraps to decorate.
   Brush with egg and bake for
   45 minutes, or until the pastry
   is golden and has risen.

Rabbit Pie

Preparation time: 45 minutes +
    overnight soaking + chilling
Total cooking time: 2 hours
    45 minutes
Serves 4

1 tablespoon vinegar
½ teaspoon salt
1 rabbit, cut into 12 portions
3 tablespoons plain (all-purpose)
    flour, seasoned with salt and pepper
4 tablespoons olive oil
2 rashers bacon, chopped
2 onions, finely chopped
1 green apple, peeled, cored and
    chopped
12 pitted prunes
1 tablespoon plain (all-purpose) flour
1 tablespoon soft brown sugar
375 ml (12 fl oz) beer or cider
1 teaspoon dried thyme
375 g (12 oz) puff pastry
1 egg yolk mixed with 1 teaspoon
    water, to glaze

1 Add the vinegar and salt to a
large bowl of water. Add the
rabbit portions and leave to soak
overnight in the fridge. Drain
and rinse well. Dry with paper
towels. Toss the rabbit in the
seasoned flour.

2 Preheat the oven to 180°C
(350°F/Gas 4). Heat 3
tablespoons of the olive oil in a
large heavy-based frying pan.
Cook the rabbit quickly, in
batches, over medium heat until
browned. Put in an 8 cup (2 litre)
casserole dish.

3 Heat the remaining oil in the
same frying pan and add the
bacon, onion, apple and prunes.

Cook over medium heat for
5 minutes or until lightly
browned. Sprinkle with the flour
and brown sugar and stir. Cook,
stirring, for 5 minutes. Add the
beer or cider and stir constantly
for 3 minutes or until thickened.
Stir in the thyme. Pour over the
rabbit. Cover the dish with a
tight-fitting lid. Bake for 2 hours
or until the rabbit is tender.

4 Transfer to a deep 5 cup (1.25
litre) pie dish with a rim. Leave to
cool and then refrigerate until
cold. Place a pie funnel in the
centre of the dish. Roll the pastry
out to about 5 cm (2 inches)
larger than the top of the pie
dish. Cut small pieces of pastry to
fit around the pie funnel. Mark
the pastry to lid size and cut out a

hole to fit over the pie funnel.
Use the remaining scraps to cut
small strips to fit on the rim of
the pie plate. Press the joins
together. Brush the pie plate rim
and strips with egg and water
glaze, position the pastry lid and
press to seal. Use the back of a
knife to push up the pastry edge
at intervals. Refrigerate for at least
30 minutes. Brush the pastry top
with egg glaze. Increase the oven
to 210°C (415°F/Gas 6–7). Bake
for 30–40 minutes or until the
pastry is golden brown and
cooked through. Reduce the oven
temperature to 180°C (350°F/
Gas 4) during the last 10 minutes
of cooking and cover with foil
to prevent the top browning
too much.

Picnic Pork Pies

Preparation time: 20 minutes
Total cooking time: 1 hour 15 minutes
Makes 6

400 g (13 oz) pork mince
¼ cup (35 g) shelled pistachios, chopped
½ apple, finely chopped
1 teaspoon finely chopped fresh sage leaves
2¼ cups (280 g) plain (all-purpose) flour
80 g (2¾ oz) butter
1 egg, lightly beaten
1 egg yolk
½ cup (125 ml) vegetable stock
½ cup (125 ml) unsweetened apple juice
1½ teaspoons gelatine

1 Preheat the oven to 200°C (400°F/ Gas 6). Combine the mince, pistachios, apple and sage in a large bowl and season very well. Fry a teaspoon of the filling and adjust the seasoning if necessary. Cover and refrigerate until needed.

2 Put the flour and ½ teaspoon of salt in a large bowl and make a well in the centre. Put the butter in a small pan with ⅓ cup (80 ml) of water and bring to the boil. Pour into the centre of the well, add the beaten egg and mix to form a smooth dough.

3 Grease six ⅓ cup (80 ml) muffin holes. Set aside one third of the dough and divide the rest into six portions. Roll each portion into a small circle and line the muffin cups with the dough, leaving a little dough hanging over the side of each cup. Divide the filling among the pastry-filled cups, packing the filling down and making a small dome shape in the centre – the filling will shrink as it cooks. Divide the remaining dough into six portions and roll each into a small circle to make the lids. Brush the edges with water and lay one on top of each pie. Fold up the pastry hanging over the edge and roll or crimp it. Cut a small hole in the top of each pie. Brush with the egg yolk mixed with a tablespoon of water.

4 Put the muffin tin on a baking tray (sheet) and bake for 30 minutes; then check the pastry top. If they are still pale, bake for another 5–10 minutes. Leave to rest for 5 minutes, then lift the pies out of the muffin tray, put them on the baking tray and bake for 15 minutes, or until the sides of the pies are golden brown (be careful not to break the pies when you move them).

5 Bring the stock and half the apple juice to the boil in a small pan. Sprinkle the gelatine over the surface of the remaining apple juice and leave to go spongy, then pour on the boiling stock and mix until the gelatine dissolves. Place a small funnel (a piping nozzle works well) in the hole of each pie and pour in a little of the gelatine mixture. Leave to settle, then pour in a little more until the pies are full. It is important to fill the pies completely to make sure there are no gaps when the gelatine mixture sets. You may need more or less liquid, depending on how much the meat shrinks. Allow to cool completely before serving.

Family-Style Meat Pie

*Preparation time: 30 minutes +
  cooling + 20 minutes
  refrigeration*
*Total cooking time: 1 hour
  45 minutes*
Serves 6

1 tablespoon oil
1 onion, chopped
1 clove garlic, crushed
750 g (1½ lb) beef mince
1 cup (250 ml) beef stock
1 cup (250 ml) beer
1 tablespoon tomato paste
1 tablespoon vegetable yeast extract
1 tablespoon Worcestershire sauce
2 teaspoons cornflour (cornstarch)
375 g (12 oz) shortcrust pastry
375 g (12 oz) puff pastry
1 egg, lightly beaten, to glaze

1 Heat the oil in a large saucepan
over medium heat and cook the
onion for 5 minutes, or until
golden. Increase the heat to
high, add the garlic and mince
and cook, breaking up any
lumps, for about 5 minutes, or
until the mince changes colour.

2 Add the stock, beer, tomato paste,
yeast extract, Worcestershire
sauce and ½ cup (125 ml) water.
Reduce the heat to medium and
cook for 1 hour, or until there is
little liquid left. Combine the
cornflour (cornstarch) with
1 tablespoon water, then stir
into the mince and cook for
5 minutes, or until thick and
glossy. Remove from the heat
and cool completely.

3 Lightly grease an 18 cm (7 inch)
pie tin. Roll the shortcrust
pastry out between two sheets of
baking paper until large enough
to line the base and side of the
tin. Use a small ball of pastry to
help press the pastry into the
tin, allowing any excess to hang
over the side of the tin.

4 Roll out the puff pastry between
two sheets of baking paper to
make a 24 cm (9 inch) circle.
Spoon the filling into the pastry
shell and smooth it down. Brush
the pastry edges with beaten
egg, then place the puff pastry

over the top. Cut off any excess
with a sharp knife. Press the top
and bottom pastries together,
then scallop the edges with a
fork or your fingers, and
refrigerate for 20 minutes.
Preheat the oven to 200°C
(400°F/Gas 6) and heat a baking
tray (sheet).

5 Brush the remaining egg over
the top of the pie, place on
the hot tray on the bottom
shelf of the oven and bake for
25–30 minutes, or until golden
and well puffed.

Beef, Stout and Potato Pie

Preparation time: 30 minutes
Total cooking time: 3 hours
 10 minutes
Serves 6

2 tablespoons olive oil
1.25 kg (2 lb 8 oz) chuck steak, cut
 into small cubes
2 onions, sliced
2 rashers bacon, roughly chopped
4 cloves garlic, crushed
2 tablespoons plain
 (all-purpose) flour
440 ml (14 fl oz) can stout
1½ cups (375 ml) beef stock
1½ tablespoons chopped
 fresh thyme
2 large potatoes, thinly sliced

1 Heat 1 tablespoon of the oil
over high heat in a large
flameproof casserole dish. Add
the beef in batches and cook,
stirring, for 5 minutes, or until
the meat is browned. Remove
from the dish. Reduce the heat
to low, add the remaining oil,
then cook the onion and bacon
for 10 minutes, stirring
occasionally. Add the garlic and
cook for another minute. Return
the beef to the casserole dish.

2 Sprinkle the flour over the beef,
cook for a minute, stirring, and
then gradually add the stout,
stirring constantly. Add the

stock, increase the heat to
medium–high and bring to the
boil. Stir in the thyme, season
well, then reduce the heat and
simmer for 2 hours, or until the
beef is tender and the mixture
has thickened.

3 Preheat the oven to 200°C
(400°F/Gas 6). Lightly grease a
5 cup (1.25 litre) ovenproof dish
and pour in the beef filling.
Arrange potato slices in a single
overlapping layer over the top to
cover the meat. Brush lightly
with olive oil and sprinkle with
salt. Bake for 30–40 minutes, or
until golden.

Raised Pork Pie

Preparation time: 20 minutes + chilling + overnight setting
Total cooking time: 1 hour
Serves 6

1.2 kg (2 lb 7 oz) minced pork
⅔ cup (90 g) pistachio nuts, shelled
  and chopped
2 green apples, peeled and finely chopped
6 fresh sage leaves, finely chopped
4 cups (500 g) plain (all-purpose) flour
150 g (5 oz) butter
2 eggs, lightly beaten
1 egg yolk, to glaze
200 ml (6½ fl oz) vegetable stock
200 ml (6½ fl oz) unsweetened apple juice
2 teaspoons gelatine

1   Preheat the oven to 200°C (400°F/
    Gas 6). Mix together the pork,
    pistachio nuts, apple and sage leaves
    and season. Fry a piece of the mixture
    to taste and adjust the seasoning.
    Cover and refrigerate. Wrap a piece of
    plastic wrap around a 6 cm (2½ inch)
    high, 20 cm (8 inch) straight-sided tin,
    then turn the tin over and grease the
    outside base and side.

2   Put the flour and 1 teaspoon salt in a
    bowl and make a well in the centre. Put
    the butter in a pan with 210 ml (7 fl oz)
    water, bring to the boil and add to the
    flour with the eggs. Mix with a wooden
    spoon until combined, then turn out
    onto a work surface and bring together
    to form a smooth dough. Wrap in plastic
    and refrigerate for 10 minutes.

3   Cut off a third of the pastry and wrap in
    plastic wrap – do not refrigerate. Roll the
    remainder into a circle large enough to
    just cover the outside of the tin. Lift onto
    a rolling pin and place over the tin,

working fast before the pastry sets.
Refrigerate until the pastry hardens.
Carefully pull out the tin and remove the
plastic wrap. Attach a paper collar made
of two layers of greased baking paper
around the outside of the pastry so it fits
snugly and secure with a paper clip at the
top and bottom. Fill the pie, then roll out
the remaining pastry to form a lid. Attach
it to the base with some water, pressing or
crimping it to make it look neat. Cut a
small hole in the top of the pie.

4   Put the pie on a baking tray (sheet),
    bake for 40 minutes and check the
    pastry top. If it is still pale, bake for
    another 10 minutes, then remove the
    paper. Brush with egg yolk mixed with
    1 tablespoon water and bake for
    another 15 minutes, or until the sides
    are brown. Cool completely.

5   Bring the stock and half the apple juice
    to the boil. Sprinkle the gelatine over
    the surface of the remaining apple juice
    in a jug and leave to go spongy, then
    pour into the stock and mix until the
    gelatine dissolves. Place a small funnel
    (a piping nozzle works well) in the hole
    of the pie and pour in a little of the
    gelatine, leave to settle and then pour in
    some more until the pie is full. Fill the
    pie completely so there are no gaps
    when the gelatine sets. Leave in the
    fridge overnight.

Grandma's Tip

*If wrapped tightly with plastic wrap,
pork pies will last in the fridge
for 4–5 days.*

Tomato and Bacon Quiche

*Preparation time: 45 minutes +
  1 hour refrigeration
Total cooking time: 1 hour
  10 minutes
Serves 6*

1½ cups (185 g) plain
  (all-purpose) flour
pinch of cayenne pepper
pinch of mustard powder
125 g (4 oz) butter, chilled
  and cubed
⅓ cup (40 g) grated cheddar
  (American) cheese
1 egg yolk

Filling

25 g (¾ oz) butter
100 g (3½ oz) lean bacon, chopped
1 small onion, finely sliced
3 eggs
¾ cup (185 ml) cream
½ teaspoon salt

2 tomatoes, peeled, seeded and
  chopped into chunks
¾ cup (90 g) grated cheddar
  (American) cheese

1 Mix the flour, pepper, mustard
   and butter in a food processor
   until crumbly. Add the cheese
   and egg yolk and process in short
   bursts until the mixture comes
   together. Add 1–2 tablespoons of
   cold water if needed. Turn out
   onto a floured surface and gather
   into a ball. Wrap in plastic and
   refrigerate for 30 minutes. Grease
   a 23 cm (9 inch) loose-based
   deep tart tin.

2 To make the filling, melt the
   butter in a frying pan and cook
   the bacon for a few minutes
   until golden. Add the onion and

cook until soft. Remove from
the heat. Lightly beat the eggs,
cream and salt together. Add the
bacon and onion, then fold in
the tomato and cheddar
(American) cheese.

3 Roll out the pastry on a floured
   surface until large enough to fit
   the tin. Trim the excess pastry
   and refrigerate for 30 minutes.
   Preheat the oven to 180°C
   (350°F/Gas 4). Cover the pastry
   with baking paper and spread
   with a layer of baking beads or
   rice. Bake for 10 minutes.
   Remove the paper and beads
   and bake for 10 minutes.

4 Pour the filling into the pastry
   shell and bake for 35 minutes
   until golden.

Quiche Lorraine

Preparation time: 35 minutes +
35 minutes refrigeration
Total cooking time: 1 hour 5 minutes
Serves 4–6

1½ cups (185 g) plain (all-purpose)
  flour
90 g (3 oz) butter, chilled and cubed
1 egg yolk
2–3 tablespoons iced water

Filling
20 g (¾ oz) butter
1 onion, chopped
4 rashers bacon, cut into thin strips
2 tablespoons chopped chives
2 eggs
¾ cup (185 ml) cream
¼ cup (60 ml) milk
100 g (3½ oz) Swiss cheese, grated

1 Mix the flour and butter in a
   food processor for 15 seconds, or
   until crumbly. Add the egg yolk
   and water. Process in short bursts
   until the mixture just comes
   together. Add a little more water
   if needed. Turn out onto a
   floured surface and gather
   together into a ball. Wrap the
   dough in plastic and refrigerate
   for at least 15 minutes.

2 Roll the pastry between two
   sheets of baking paper until large
   enough to line a shallow 25 cm
   (10 inch) loose-based tart tin.
   Press well into the side of the tin
   and trim off any excess pastry.
   Refrigerate the pastry-lined tin
   for 20 minutes. Preheat the oven
   to 190°C (375°F/Gas 5).

3 Cover the pastry shell with
   baking paper, spread with a layer
   of baking beads or rice and bake
   for 15 minutes. Remove the paper
   and beads and bake the pastry
   shell for 10 minutes, or until the
   pastry is golden and dry. Reduce
   the oven temperature to 180°C
   (350°F/Gas 4).

4 To make the filling, heat the
   butter in a pan. Add the onion
   and bacon and cook for

10 minutes, stirring frequently,
until the onion is soft and the
bacon is cooked. Stir through
the chives and leave to cool.

5 Beat together the eggs, cream
   and milk. Season with pepper.
   Spread the onion and bacon
   filling evenly into the pastry
   shell. Pour the egg mixture over
   the top and sprinkle with the
   cheese. Bake for 30 minutes, or
   until the filling is set and golden.

Tomato and Thyme Quiche

Preparation time: 35 minutes +
*   30 minutes refrigeration*
Total cooking time: 45 minutes
Serves 8

1½ cups (185 g) plain
   (all-purpose) flour
125 g (4 oz) butter, chilled and cubed
1 egg yolk
2–3 tablespoons iced water

Filling
425 g (14 oz) can tomatoes
4 eggs
300 g (10 oz) sour cream
¼ cup (25 g) grated parmesan
2 spring (green) onions,
   finely chopped
1–2 tablespoons chopped fresh thyme

1 Preheat the oven to 210°C (415°F/
   Gas 6–7). Sift the flour into a bowl
   and rub in the butter until the mixture
   resembles fine breadcrumbs. Add the
   combined egg yolk and water and mix
   to a soft dough. Turn out onto a
   lightly floured surface and gather into
   a ball. Wrap in plastic and refrigerate
   for 30 minutes.

2 Roll out the pastry to line a shallow
   23 cm (9 inch) tart tin, trimming off
   the excess. Cover with baking paper
   and spread with a layer of baking beads
   or rice. Bake for 10 minutes, then
   discard the paper and beads and cook
   for a further 5 minutes or until golden.

3 Drain the tomatoes and halve
   lengthways. Place, cut-side-down, on
   paper towels to drain. Beat together
   the eggs and sour cream and stir in the
   cheese and spring (green) onion.

4 Pour the filling into the pastry shell.
   Arrange the tomatoes, cut-side-down,
   over the filling. Sprinkle with thyme
   and pepper. Reduce the oven to 180°C
   (350°F/Gas 4) and bake for 30 minutes
   or until the filling is set and golden.

Grandma's Note

The pastry shell can be blind baked a
day in advance and stored in an
airtight container.

Steak and Kidney Pie

Preparation time: 20 minutes
Total cooking time: 2 hours
Serves 6

750 g (1 lb 8 oz) round steak
4 lamb kidneys
2 tablespoons plain (all-purpose) flour
1 tablespoon oil
1 onion, chopped
30 g (1 oz) butter
1 tablespoon Worcestershire sauce
1 tablespoon tomato paste
½ cup (125 ml) red wine
1 cup (250 ml) beef stock
125 g (4 oz) button
  mushrooms, sliced
½ teaspoon dried thyme
⅓ cup (20 g) chopped fresh parsley
375 g (12 oz) puff pastry
1 egg, lightly beaten, to glaze

1 Cut the meat into small cubes. Trim the skin from the kidneys. Quarter the kidneys and trim away any fat or sinew. Coat the meat and kidneys with the flour and shake off the excess.

2 Heat the oil in a pan. Add the onion and cook for 5 minutes, or until soft. Remove with a slotted spoon. Add the butter to the pan. Brown the meat and kidneys in batches and then return all the meat and onion to the pan.

3 Add the Worcestershire sauce, tomato paste, wine, beef stock, sliced mushrooms, thyme and parsley to the pan. Bring to the boil, then simmer, covered, for 1 hour or until the meat is tender. Season and leave to cool. Spoon into a 6 cup (1.5 litre) pie dish.

4 Preheat the oven to 210°C (415°F/Gas 6–7). Roll the puff pastry out on a lightly floured surface so that it is 5 cm (2 inches) larger than the dish. Cut thin strips from the pastry and press onto the rim, sealing the joins. Place the pastry on top of the pie. Trim the edges and cut steam holes in the top. Decorate with pastry trimmings and brush the top with egg. Bake for 35–40 minutes or until golden brown.

Cornish Pasties

Preparation time: 1 hour + chilling
Total cooking time: 45 minutes
Makes 6

2½ cups (310 g) plain
  (all-purpose) flour
125 g (4 oz) butter, chilled and cubed
4–5 tablespoons iced water
160 g (5½ oz) round steak, diced
1 small potato, finely chopped
1 small onion, finely chopped
1 small carrot, finely chopped
1–2 teaspoons Worcestershire sauce
2 tablespoons beef stock
1 egg, lightly beaten

1 Grease a baking tray (sheet). Mix the flour, butter and a pinch of salt in a food processor for 15 seconds, or until crumbly. Add the water and process in short bursts until it comes together. Turn out onto a floured surface and form into a ball. Wrap in plastic and chill for 30 minutes. Preheat the oven to 210°C (415°F/Gas 6–7).

2 Mix together the steak, potato, onion, carrot, Worcestershire sauce and stock. Season well.

3 Divide the dough into six portions and roll out to 3 mm (⅛ inch) thick. Cut into six 16 cm (6½ inch) rounds. Divide the filling evenly and put in the centre of each pastry circle.

4 Brush the pastry edges with egg and fold over. Pinch to form a frill and place on the tray. Brush with egg and bake for 15 minutes. Lower the heat to 180°C (350°F/Gas 4) and bake for 25–30 minutes, or until golden.

Rich Beef Pie

Preparation time: 35 minutes + chilling
Total cooking time: 2 hours 45 minutes
Serves 6

Filling
2 tablespoons oil
1 kg (2 lb) chuck steak, cubed
1 large onion, chopped
1 large carrot, finely chopped
2 cloves garlic, crushed
2 tablespoons plain (all-purpose) flour
1 cup (250 ml) beef stock
2 teaspoons fresh thyme leaves
1 tablespoon Worcestershire sauce

Pastry
2 cups (250 g) plain (all-purpose) flour
150 g (5 oz) butter, chilled and cubed
1 egg yolk
3–4 tablespoons iced water
1 egg yolk and 1 tablespoon milk, to glaze

1 Heat 1 tablespoon of the oil in a large pan and brown the meat in batches. Remove all the meat from the pan and set aside. Heat the remaining oil, then add the onion, carrot and garlic and cook over medium heat until browned.

2 Return all the meat to the pan and stir in the flour. Cook for 1 minute, then remove from the heat and slowly stir in the beef stock, mixing the flour in well. Add the thyme leaves and Worcestershire sauce, and bring to the boil. Season to taste.

3 Reduce the heat to very low, cover and simmer for 1½–2 hours, or until the meat is tender. During the last 15 minutes of cooking remove the lid and allow the liquid to reduce until very thick. Cool completely.

4 To make the pastry, sift the flour into a large bowl and add the butter. Using your fingertips, rub the butter into the flour until it resembles fine breadcrumbs. Add the egg yolk and 2 tablespoons of iced water, and mix with a knife using a cutting action until the mixture comes together in beads, adding a little more water if necessary. Turn out onto a lightly floured surface and gather together to form a smooth dough. Wrap in plastic wrap and refrigerate for 30 minutes.

5 Preheat the oven to 200°C (400°F/Gas 6). Divide the pastry into two pieces and roll out one of the pieces on a sheet of baking paper until large enough to line a 23 cm (9 inch) pie dish. Line the pie dish with the pastry. Fill with the cold filling and roll out the remaining piece of pastry until large enough to fully cover the dish. Dampen the edges of the pastry with your fingers dipped in water. Lay the top piece of pastry over the pie and gently press the bottom and top pieces of pastry together. Trim the overhanging edges with a sharp knife and re-roll the trimmings to make decorations for the pie top.

6 Cut a few slits in the top of the pastry to allow the steam to escape. Beat together the egg yolk and milk, and brush it over the top of the pie. Cook in the oven for 20–30 minutes, or until the pastry is golden.

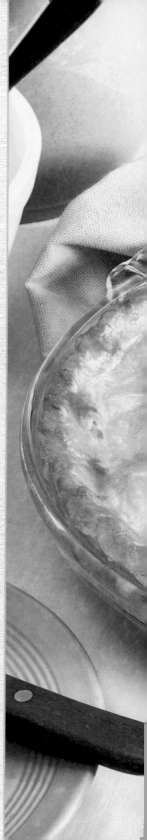

Spinach Pie

Preparation time: 30 minutes +
*   30 minutes chilling*
Total cooking time: 1 hour
Serves 8–10

2 cups (250 g) plain (all-purpose) flour
⅓ cup (80 ml) olive oil
1 egg, beaten
4–5 tablespoons iced water

Filling

1 kg (2 lb) spinach, stalks removed,
    roughly chopped
1 tablespoon olive oil
1 large leek, sliced
4 cloves garlic, crushed
2 cups (500 g) ricotta
1 cup (90 g) grated pecorino cheese
300 g (10 oz) feta, crumbled
3 eggs, lightly beaten
3 tablespoons chopped fresh dill
½ cup (15 g) chopped fresh
    flat-leaf parsley

1 Sift the flour and ½ teaspoon salt into a large bowl and make a well in the centre. Mix the oil, egg and most of the water, add to the flour and mix with a flat-bladed knife until the mixture comes together in beads, adding a little more water if necessary. Gather the dough and press into a ball. Wrap in plastic wrap and chill for at least 30 minutes.

2 Put the spinach in a large pan, sprinkle lightly with water, then cover and steam for 5 minutes until wilted. Drain, squeeze out the excess moisture, then finely chop.

3 Preheat the oven to 200°C (400°F/ Gas 6) and heat a baking tray (sheet). Grease a 25 cm (12 inch) loose-based fluted tart tin. Heat

the oil in a frying pan and cook the leek and garlic over low heat for 5 minutes, or until soft. Mix with the ricotta, pecorino, feta, spinach, egg, dill and parsley and season with salt and pepper.

4 Roll out two-thirds of the pastry between two sheets of baking paper until large enough to line the tin. Fill with the spinach mixture. Roll out the remaining pastry between the baking paper and top the pie. Trim the edges and make two or three steam holes.

5 Bake the pie on the hot tray for 15 minutes, then reduce the oven to 180°C (350°F/Gas 4) and cook for another 30 minutes. Cover with foil if the pie is overbrowning. Leave for 5–10 minutes before slicing.

Bacon and Egg Pie

Preparation time: 20 minutes + chilling
Total cooking time: 1 hour
Serves 4–6

1 sheet shortcrust pastry
2 teaspoons oil
4 rashers bacon, chopped
5 eggs, lightly beaten
¼ cup (60 ml) cream
1 sheet puff pastry
1 egg, lightly beaten, to glaze

1   Preheat the oven to 210°C (415°F/Gas 6–7). Lightly oil a 20 cm (8 inch) loose-bottomed flan tin. Place the shortcrust pastry in the tin and trim the pastry edges. Cut a sheet of greaseproof paper to cover the pastry-lined tin. Spread a layer of baking beads, dried beans or rice over the paper. Bake for 10 minutes and then discard the paper and beads. Bake the pastry for another 5–10 minutes or until golden. Allow to cool.

2   Heat the oil in a frying pan. Add the bacon and cook over medium heat for a few minutes or until lightly browned. Drain on paper towels and allow to cool slightly. Arrange the bacon over the pastry base and pour the mixed eggs and cream over the top.

3   Brush the edges of the pastry with the egg glaze, cover with puff pastry and press on firmly to seal. Trim the pastry edges and decorate the top with trimmings. Brush with egg glaze and bake for 30–35 minutes, or until puffed and golden.

Soups

Only the pure in heart can make a good soup.

Ludwig Van Beethoven

Cream of Tomato Soup

Preparation time: 25 minutes
Total cooking time: 30 minutes
Serves 4

1.25 kg (2½ lb) tomatoes
1 tablespoon oil
1 onion, chopped
1 clove garlic, chopped
1½ cups (375 ml) chicken stock
2 tablespoons tomato paste
1 teaspoon sugar
1 cup (250 ml) cream

1 Cut a cross in the base of each tomato. Cover with boiling water for 1 minute, plunge in iced water, drain and peel away the skins. Scoop out the seeds and discard, then roughly chop the flesh.

2 Heat the oil in a large pan and cook the onion for 3 minutes, or until soft. Add the garlic and cook for 1 minute longer. Add the tomato and cook for 5 minutes, stirring occasionally, until very soft. Stir in the stock, bring to the boil, reduce the heat and simmer for 10 minutes.

3 Cool slightly, then transfer to a food processor. Process in batches until smooth, and return to the pan. Add the tomato paste and sugar and bring to the boil, stirring continuously. Reduce the heat and stir in the cream but do not allow the soup to boil. Season to taste before serving. Serve with an extra spoonful of cream and chopped parsley, if you like.

Grandma's Tips

It is best to use plump, ripe tomatoes for this recipe.

If you are not using home-made stock, remember to taste the soup before seasoning. Shop-bought stock can be very salty.

Leek and Potato Soup

Preparation time: 15 minutes
Total cooking time: 30 minutes
Serves 4

4 leeks, trimmed and cut into
   4 lengthways
30 g (1 oz) butter
3 floury potatoes, chopped
3 cups (750 ml) chicken or
   vegetable stock
1 cup (250 ml) milk
¼ teaspoon ground nutmeg
cream and chopped fresh spring
   (green) onions, to garnish

1 Wash the leeks thoroughly in
cold water to remove any dirt,
then cut into small chunks. Heat
the butter in a large saucepan.
Add the leek and cook for 3–4
minutes, stirring frequently,
until softened. Add the potato
and stock. Bring slowly to the
boil, then reduce the heat and
simmer for 20 minutes, or until
the vegetables are tender.

2 Cool the mixture slightly then
transfer to a blender or food
processor and purée in batches.
Return to the pan, stir in the
milk and nutmeg, and season
well with salt and ground black
pepper. Reheat gently and serve
garnished with a swirl of cream
and a scattering of spring
(green) onion.

Grandma's Tip

*Use old floury potatoes such as
sebago for the best results.*

Roast Pumpkin Soup

Preparation time: 20 minutes
Total cooking time: 55 minutes
Serves 6

1.25 kg (2 lb 12 oz) butternut pumpkin (squash),
   peeled and cut into chunks
2 tablespoons olive oil
1 large onion, chopped
2 teaspoons ground cumin
1 large carrot, chopped
1 celery stalk, chopped
4 cups (1 litre) chicken or vegetable stock
sour cream, to serve
finely chopped parsley, to serve
ground nutmeg, to serve

1 Preheat the oven to 180°C (350°F/Gas 4). Put the pumpkin on a greased baking tray
   (sheet) and lightly brush with half the olive oil. Bake for 25 minutes, or until softened
   and slightly browned around the edges.

2 Heat the remaining oil in a large pan. Cook the onion and cumin for 2 minutes, then
   add the carrot and celery and cook for 3 minutes more, stirring frequently. Add the
   roasted pumpkin and stock. Bring to the boil, then reduce the heat and simmer for
   20 minutes.

3 Allow to cool a little, then purée in batches in a blender or food processor. Return the
   soup to the pan and gently reheat without boiling. Season to taste with salt and
   ground black pepper. Top with sour cream and sprinkle with chopped parsley and
   ground nutmeg before serving.

Grandma's Note

*Butternut pumpkin (squash) has
a sweeter flavour than
other varieties.*

Country Lentil, Bacon and Garlic Soup

Preparation time: 35 minutes
Total cooking time: 1 hour 5 minutes
Serves 4–6

¼ cup (60 ml) olive oil
3 onions, finely chopped
6 cloves garlic, thinly sliced
150 g (5 oz) bacon, finely chopped
3 carrots, finely chopped
2 parsnips, finely chopped
3 sticks celery, sliced
200 g (6½ oz) red lentils, rinsed
4 cups (1 litre) vegetable stock
¼ cup (60 g) tomato paste
¼ cup (65 g) risoni (rice-shaped pasta)
4 spring (green) onions, finely chopped
¼ cup (15 g) chopped parsley
2 teaspoons finely grated lemon rind
100 g (3½ oz) grated parmesan, to serve

1 Heat the oil in a large pan. Add the
   onion, garlic and bacon and cook, stirring
   occasionally, over low–medium heat for
   15 minutes, or until a deep golden brown.

2 Add the carrot, parsnip and celery, stir
   well, cover and cook for 5 minutes, or
   until softened. Stir in the lentils, stock,
   tomato paste and 4 cups (1 litre) of water.
   Bring to the boil, reduce the heat and
   simmer, uncovered, for 30 minutes, or
   until the lentils are tender; skim the
   surface as required.

3 Stir in the risoni and 2 cups (500 ml) of
   water. Return to the boil and simmer for
   10 minutes.

4 Add the spring (green) onion, parsley and
   lemon rind and season to taste. Serve with
   the grated parmesan.

Chicken and Corn Soup

Preparation time: 15 minutes
Total cooking time: 20 minutes
Serves 6

3 corn cobs
1 tablespoon vegetable oil
4 spring (green) onions, finely chopped
2 teaspoons grated ginger
4 cups (1 litre) chicken stock
1 tablespoon rice wine, mirin or sherry
1 tablespoon light soy sauce
½ small barbecued chicken, shredded
1 tablespoon cornflour (cornstarch)
1 teaspoon sesame oil
420 g (15 oz) can creamed corn
  (corn, cream-style)
thyme sprigs, to garnish

1 Cut the corn kernels from the cobs – you will need about 2 cups (400 g). Heat the oil in a large pan, and add the spring (green) onion and ginger. Cook for 1 minute, or until softened, then add the corn, stock, rice wine and soy sauce. Bring slowly to the boil, then reduce the heat and simmer for 10 minutes, or until the kernels are cooked through. Add the chicken.

2 In a bowl, blend the cornflour (cornstarch) with 3 tablespoons water or stock to make a smooth paste. Add to the soup with the sesame oil and simmer, stirring continuously, until slightly thickened. Stir in the corn and heat for 2–3 minutes without allowing to boil. Season with salt and ground black pepper and serve hot, garnished with thyme sprigs.

Scotch Broth

Preparation time: 40 minutes +
  1 hour soaking + overnight
  refrigeration
Total cooking time: 4 hours
Serves 8

1 kg (2 lb) lamb shanks, cut in
  half through the bone (ask your
  butcher to do this)
3 onions, chopped
3 turnips, chopped
2 carrots, chopped
1 tablespoon black peppercorns
½ cup (110 g) pearl barley
1 carrot, diced, extra
2 onions, finely chopped, extra
1 leek, chopped
1 stick celery, diced
2 turnips, diced, extra
chopped flat-leaf parsley

1 To make the stock, put the lamb
shanks, onion, turnip, carrot,
peppercorns and 8 cups (2 litres)
of water in a large pan. Bring to
the boil, reduce the heat and
simmer, covered, for 3 hours.
Skim the surface as required.

2 Remove the shanks and any
meat that has fallen off the
bones and cool slightly. Remove
the meat from the bones and
finely chop, then cover and
refrigerate. Strain the stock,
discarding the vegetables.
Cool the stock and refrigerate
overnight, or until the fat has set
on top and can be spooned off.
Cover the barley with water and
soak for 1 hour.

3 Put the stock in a large pan and
gently reheat. Add the drained
barley, extra carrot, onion, leek,
celery and turnip. Bring to the
boil, reduce the heat and
simmer for 30 minutes, or until
the barley and vegetables are just
cooked. Return the meat to the
pan and simmer for 5 minutes.
Season well and serve with
the parsley.

Pea and Ham Soup

Preparation time: 15 minutes +
overnight soaking
Total cooking time: 2 hours
Serves 8

500 g (1 lb 2 oz) split peas
1 leek
1 tablespoon oil
2 carrots, chopped
1 celery stalk, chopped
2 garlic cloves, crushed
750 g (1 lb 10 oz) meaty ham bone

1 Put the split peas in a large bowl, completely cover with water and soak overnight.

2 Cut the leek in half lengthways and wash thoroughly in cold water to remove any dirt. Slice thickly. Heat the oil in a large saucepan, and add the leek, carrot, celery and garlic. Cook, stirring, for 2–3 minutes, then add the drained peas, the ham bone and 10 cups (2.5 litres) water. Bring to the boil, then reduce the heat and simmer for 2 hours, stirring occasionally.

3 Remove the ham bone and set it aside to cool. Cool the soup a little then purée in batches in a blender or food processor and return to the pan. Remove the meat from the bone, chop and return the meat to the soup. Season to taste with salt and ground black pepper, reheat gently and serve hot.

Grandma's Note

Either yellow or green split peas can be used in this recipe.

Chicken and Vegetable Soup

Preparation time: 1 hour + refrigeration
Total cooking time: 1 hour 25 minutes
Serves 6–8

1.5 kg (2½ lb) chicken
2 carrots, roughly chopped
2 sticks celery, roughly chopped
1 onion, quartered
4 parsley sprigs
2 bay leaves
4 black peppercorns
50 g (1¾ oz) butter
2 tablespoons plain (all-purpose) flour
2 potatoes, chopped
250 g (8 oz) butternut pumpkin (squash),
　chopped into bite-sized pieces
2 carrots, extra, cut into matchsticks
1 leek, cut into matchsticks
3 sticks celery, extra, cut into matchsticks
100 g (3½ oz) green beans, cut into short
　lengths or baby green beans, halved
200 g (6½ oz) broccoli, cut into small florets
100 g (3½ oz) sugar snap peas (snow peas or
　pea pods), trimmed
50 g (1¾ oz) English spinach
　leaves, shredded
½ cup (125 ml) cream
¼ cup (15 g) chopped parsley

1 To make the chicken stock, place the
chicken in a large pan with the carrot,
celery, onion, parsley, bay leaves,
2 teaspoons of salt and the
peppercorns. Add 3 litres of water.
Bring to the boil, reduce the heat
and simmer for 1 hour, skimming
the surface as required. Allow to cool
for at least 30 minutes. Strain and
reserve the liquid.

2 Remove the chicken and allow to cool
enough to handle. Discard the skin,
then cut or pull the flesh from the
bones and shred into small pieces. Set
the chicken meat aside.

3 Heat the butter in a large pan over
medium heat and, when foaming, add
the flour. Cook, stirring, for
1 minute. Remove from the heat and
gradually stir in the stock. Return
to the heat and bring to the boil,
stirring continuously. Add the potato,
pumpkin (squash) and extra carrot and
simmer for 7 minutes. Add the leek,
extra celery and beans and simmer for
a further 5 minutes. Finally, add the
broccoli and peas and cook for a
further 3 minutes.

4 Just before serving, add the chicken
meat, spinach, cream and chopped
parsley. Reheat gently but do not allow
the soup to boil. Keep stirring until the
spinach has wilted. Season to taste with
plenty of salt and freshly ground black
pepper. Serve immediately.

Grandma's Note

*The chicken stock (up to the end of Step 1)
can be made 1 day ahead and kept,
covered, in the refrigerator. This can, in
fact, be beneficial – before reheating
the stock, spoon off the fat which will
have formed on the surface.*

Minestrone

Preparation time: 30 minutes
Total cooking time: 2 hours
   30 minutes
Serves 8

1 tablespoon olive oil
1 onion, finely chopped
2 garlic cloves, crushed
2 carrots, diced
2 potatoes, diced
2 celery stalks, finely chopped
2 zucchinis (courgettes),
   finely chopped
125 g (4½ oz) green beans, chopped
2 cups (150 g) shredded cabbage

8 cups (2 litres) beef stock
425 g (15 oz) can chopped tomatoes
½ cup (80 g) macaroni
440 g (1 lb) can borlotti (pinto) or
   red kidney beans, drained
grated parmesan cheese, to serve
thyme sprigs, to serve

1 Heat the oil in a large saucepan.
   Add the onion and garlic
   and cook over low heat for
   5 minutes. Add the carrot,
   potato and celery and cook,
   stirring constantly, for a further
   5 minutes.

2 Add the zucchini (courgette),
   green beans and cabbage to
   the pan and cook, stirring, for
   5 minutes. Add the stock and
   chopped tomatoes. Bring slowly
   to the boil, then reduce the heat,
   cover and leave to simmer for
   2 hours.

3 Add the macaroni and beans,
   and cook for 15 minutes, or
   until pasta is tender. Serve hot
   with a generous sprinkling of
   parmesan and garnish with a
   sprig of fresh thyme.

Oxtail Soup

Preparation time: 20 minutes +
   chilling
Total cooking time: 3 hours
   20 minutes
Serves 4

2 tablespoons plain (all-purpose) flour
1 kg (2 lb 4 oz) oxtail, chopped into
   5 cm (2 inch) pieces
1 tablespoon oil
8 cups (2 litres) beef stock
1 onion, chopped
1 celery stalk, chopped
2 carrots, chopped
1 turnip, peeled and chopped
3 whole cloves
12 peppercorns
2 bay leaves
2 tablespoons port

1 tablespoon tomato paste (purée)
⅓ cup (20 g) chopped parsley

1 Season 1 tablespoon of the flour
and put it in a plastic bag with
the oxtail and shake to coat.
Shake off excess flour. Heat the
oil in a saucepan, add the oxtail
and cook in batches, tossing
continually, for 5 minutes, or
until evenly browned. Return all
the oxtail to the pan.

2 Add the stock, vegetables, cloves,
peppercorns, bay leaves,
½ teaspoon salt and 1½ cups
(375ml) water. Bring slowly to
the boil then reduce the heat and
simmer, covered, for 3 hours.

3 Strain the vegetables and meat,
reserving the liquid. Discard
the vegetables and leave the
meat to cool. Pull the meat from
the bone, shred and refrigerate.
Meanwhile, refrigerate the stock
until the fat has solidified on the
surface. Spoon the fat off and
add the meat.

4 Put the soup in a clean pan.
Mix together the remaining flour,
port and tomato paste, and add
to the pan. Bring to the boil,
stirring, until the soup thickens.
Simmer for 10 minutes, then
stir in the parsley.

Potato and Carrot Soup

Preparation time: 20 minutes
Total cooking time: 25–30 minutes
Serves 4

2 tablespoons oil
2 cloves garlic, crushed
1 onion, chopped
2 teaspoons ground cumin
1 teaspoon ground coriander
4 carrots, chopped
750 g (1½ lb) floury potatoes,
    peeled and chopped
4 cups (1 litre) vegetable stock
½ cup (125 ml) cream
sour cream and coriander (cilantro) leaves,
    to garnish

1 Heat the oil in a heavy-based pan, add the garlic and onion and cook until softened. Add the cumin, coriander and ½ teaspoon of salt and cook for another minute. Add the carrot and potato and toss to coat. Add the stock to the pan and bring to the boil.

2 Reduce the heat and simmer for 20 minutes, or until the vegetables are tender. Cool slightly.

3 Process, in batches, until smooth, then return to the pan and heat gently. Stir in the cream. Serve garnished with sour cream and coriander (cilantro) leaves.

Cream of Mushroom Soup

Preparation time: 30 minutes
Total cooking time: 15 minutes
Serves 4

500 g (1 lb) large field mushrooms
50 g (1¾ oz) butter
4 spring (green) onions, finely chopped
3 cloves garlic, finely chopped
1 teaspoon chopped lemon thyme
2 teaspoons plain (all-purpose) flour
4 cups (1 litre) chicken or vegetable stock
1 cup (250 ml) cream
chives and thyme, to garnish

1 Thinly slice the mushroom caps, discarding the stalks. Melt the butter in a heavy-based pan and cook the spring (green) onion, garlic and lemon thyme, stirring, for 1 minute, or until the garlic is golden. Add the mushroom and ½ teaspoon each of salt and white pepper. Cook for 3–4 minutes, or until the mushroom just softens. Add the flour and cook, stirring, for 1 minute.

2 Remove from the heat and add the stock, stirring continuously. Return to the heat and bring to the boil, stirring. Reduce the heat and simmer gently for 2 minutes, stirring occasionally.

3 Whisk the cream into the soup, then reheat gently, stirring. Do not allow the soup to boil. Season to taste with salt and pepper, and garnish with the chopped chives and thyme.

Cabbage and Ham Soup with Cheese Dumplings

Preparation time: 40 minutes
Total cooking time: 1 hour 10 minutes
Serves 6

¼ cup (60 ml) olive oil
350 g (11 oz) piece of double-smoked ham,
   chopped into cubes
2 teaspoons soft brown sugar
2 onions, thinly sliced
2 leeks, thinly sliced
3 cloves garlic, finely chopped
1 tablespoon plain (all-purpose) flour
2 cups (500 ml) chicken stock
250 g (8 oz) bacon bones
3 potatoes, chopped
½ savoy cabbage, finely shredded
1 tablespoon white wine vinegar

Cheese dumplings

30g (1 oz) cold butter, cut into small pieces
2 cups (250 g) self-raising flour
60 g (2 oz) finely grated cheddar
   (American) cheese
2 teaspoons finely chopped thyme
2 teaspoons finely grated lemon rind, optional

1 Heat 1 tablespoon of the oil in a large
pan and add the ham and sugar. Sauté
over high heat, stirring continuously, for
5 minutes, or until just golden. Remove
with a slotted spoon and drain on paper
towels. Take care not to overcook or the
ham will become dry.

2 Add the remaining oil, onion, leek and
garlic and cook for 15 minutes over
low heat, stirring regularly. Add the
flour and cook for 1 minute, stirring.

Remove from the heat and gradually
add the stock, bacon bones and 6 cups
(1.5 litres) of water. Return to the heat
and cook, stirring, until the mixture
comes to the boil and thickens slightly.
Reduce the heat and simmer for
30 minutes, skimming the surface
as required.

3 Remove the bacon bones, cut off the
meat and discard the bones. Shred the
meat into small pieces. Return to the
pan with the potato and simmer for
10 minutes, or until the potato is tender.
Add the ham, cabbage and vinegar and
season with pepper, cover and cook over
very low heat for 5–10 minutes while
preparing the dumplings.

4 To make the dumplings, rub the butter
into the flour until crumbly. Mix in
the cheese, thyme and about ½ cup (125
ml) of water, or enough to bind the
mixture together. Roll 2 level teaspoons
of the mixture into balls. Place into the
soup and simmer, covered, for 8 minutes,
or until the dumplings are plump. Season
to taste and scatter with the lemon rind.
Serve immediately.

Grandma's Tip

*Avoid crusty-looking bacon bones as
they are extremely salty. Taste before
adding any extra salt to
this recipe.*

Chunky Vegetable Soup

Preparation time: 25 minutes
Total cooking time: 1 hour 30 minutes
Serves 6

50 g (1¾ oz) butter
1 leek, chopped
1 celery stalk, chopped
1 large carrot, chopped
1 large potato, chopped
1 parsnip, peeled and chopped
1 swede (rutabaga) or turnip,
    peeled and chopped
225 g (8 oz) sweet potato
    (yam), chopped
½ cup (115 g) soup mix
8 cups (2 litres) vegetable
    stock or water
1 cup (155 g) frozen peas
125 g (4½ oz) green
    beans, chopped
¼ cup (15 g) chopped mint
⅓ cup (20 g) chopped parsley

1 Heat the butter in a large saucepan, and cook the leek, celery, carrot, potato, parsnip, swede (rutabaga) or turnip and sweet potato (yam), stirring, for 5 minutes.

2 Add the soup mix and stock or water. Bring slowly to the boil, then reduce the heat and simmer, covered, for 1¼ hours, or until the soup mix has softened.

3 Add the peas and beans, and cook for a further 10 minutes, or until tender. Stir in the chopped mint and parsley. Season to taste and serve hot. Delicious with crusty bread.

Grandma's Note

Soup mix is a combination
of dried beans and pulses.

Mulligatawny Soup

Preparation time: 25 minutes
Total cooking time: 1 hour 25 minutes
Serves 4–6

500 g (1 lb) chicken thigh fillets,
    excess fat removed
2 tablespoons plain (all-purpose) flour
1 tablespoon curry powder
1 teaspoon ground turmeric
30 g (1 oz) butter
1 onion, finely chopped
1 apple, peeled, cored and finely chopped
4 cups (1 litre) chicken stock
6 whole cloves, tied in muslin
⅓ cup (65 g) basmati rice
1 tablespoon lemon juice
¼ cup (60 ml) cream

1 Coat the chicken in the combined flour, curry powder and turmeric.
Heat half the butter in a large pan and cook the chicken over
medium heat for 3–4 minutes, or until lightly browned; turn
frequently. Remove from the pan and drain on paper towels.

2 Add the remaining butter to the pan, then add the onion, apple
and remaining flour mixture and cook for 3 minutes, or until soft.
Return the chicken to the pan along with the stock and cloves.
Bring to the boil, reduce the heat and simmer, covered, for 1 hour.
Add the rice during the last 15 minutes and cook until it is tender.

3 Remove the chicken; allow to cool slightly and chop finely. Remove
the cloves and skim any oil from the surface. Return the chicken to
the pan. Reheat gently, stir in the lemon juice and cream, but do
not allow the soup to boil. Season to taste with salt and freshly
ground black pepper.

Clam Chowder

Preparation time: 35 minutes
Total cooking time: 45 minutes
Serves 4

1.5 kg (3 lb) fresh clams in shell
3 rashers bacon, chopped
1 onion, chopped
1 clove garlic, crushed
4 potatoes (about 750 g/1½ lb),
    peeled and cubed
1¼ cups (315 ml) fish stock
2 cups (500 ml) milk
½ cup (125 ml) cream
3 tablespoons chopped parsley

1   Discard any clams that are
    already open (these should not
    be used). Put the rest in a large
    heavy-based pan with 1 cup
    (250 ml) of water and simmer,
    covered, over low heat for
    5 minutes, or until the shells
    open (discard any that do not
    open during cooking). Strain
    the liquid and reserve. Remove
    the clam meat from the shells.

2   Heat a little oil in the clean pan,
    add the bacon, onion and garlic
    and cook, stirring, until the onion
    is soft and the bacon golden. Add
    the potato and stir to combine.

3   Measure the reserved liquid and
    add enough water to make it up
    .to 1¼ cups (315 ml). Add to
    the pan with the stock and milk.
    Bring to the boil, reduce the
    heat, cover and simmer for
    20 minutes, or until the potato

is tender. Uncover and simmer
for 10 minutes, or until reduced
and slightly thickened.

4   Add the cream, clam meat and
    parsley and season, to taste.
    Heat through gently before
    serving, but do not allow to boil
    or it may curdle.

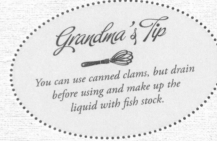

Grandma's Tip

You can use canned clams, but drain
before using and make up the
liquid with fish stock.

Smoked Haddock Chowder

Preparation time: 20 minutes
Total cooking time: 25 minutes
Serves 4

500 g (1 lb 2 oz) smoked haddock
1 leek, washed and finely chopped
1 celery stalk, finely chopped
2 potatoes, diced
50 g (1¾ oz) butter
3 tablespoons plain
  (all-purpose) flour
2 cups (500 ml) milk
¼ cup (60 ml) cream
¼ cup (15 g) chopped parsley

1 Put the haddock in a large deep frying pan and cover with water. Bring to the boil for 1 minute, then drain. Add 2 cups (500 ml) water and bring to the boil, then reduce the heat and simmer for 8 minutes. Remove the fish and drain on paper towels. Reserve the poaching liquid. Let the haddock cool, then flake, discarding the skin and bone. Cover and set aside.

2 Put the leek, celery and potato in a large saucepan. Add the poaching liquid and enough water to make it up to 3 cups (750 ml). Pour into the pan, bring to the boil, then reduce the heat and simmer for 10 minutes.

3 Meanwhile, melt the butter in a saucepan. Add the flour and cook, stirring, for 1 minute. Remove from the heat and gradually add the milk, then cook, stirring, for 2 minutes, or until it boils and thickens. Cook for 2 minutes, then add the cream, fish, vegetables, poaching liquid and parsley. Season to taste with salt and ground black pepper. Reheat without boiling and serve hot.

French Onion Soup

Preparation time: 15 minutes
Total cooking time: 1 hour 30 minutes
Serves 4–6

1 tablespoon olive oil
30 g (1 oz) butter
1 kg (2 lb) onions, thinly sliced
1½ tablespoons soft brown sugar
4 tablespoons plain (all-purpose) flour
6 cups (1.5 litres) beef stock
½ cup (125 ml) brandy
¼ cup (60 ml) olive oil, extra
2 cloves garlic, crushed
1 French bread stick
1 cup (100 g) grated parmesan cheese

1 Heat the oil and butter in a large, heavy-based pan. Add the onion and stir over low heat for 1 minute. Cover and cook for a further 20 minutes, stirring occasionally. Add the sugar and ½ teaspoon of salt and increase the heat. Cook for 30 minutes, stirring frequently, or until the onion is golden brown.

2 Gradually add the flour. Cook for 3 minutes over medium heat, stirring. Remove from the heat and gradually add the combined stock and brandy.

3 Over medium heat, bring to the boil, stirring constantly, until slightly thickened. Partially cover the saucepan, lower the heat and simmer gently for 30 minutes, stirring occasionally. Season to taste.

4 Mix the extra oil and garlic. Cut the bread stick into thick slices and toast both sides under a preheated grill (broiler), until lightly browned. Brush on the oil and sprinkle with the cheese. Grill (broil) until melted and serve on the soup.

Grandma's Note

Although it is more expensive, you can use Reggiano Parmesan for this recipe; it has an excellent creamy taste and rich, grainy texture. It is available from delicatessens.

Spring Vegetable Soup

Preparation time: 30 minutes +
  overnight soaking
Total cooking time: 1 hour
  15 minutes
Serves 8

½ cup (105 g) borlotti (pinto) beans
2 teaspoons olive oil
2 onions, finely chopped
2 cloves garlic, finely chopped
10 cups (2.5 litres) vegetable stock
2 sticks celery, finely chopped
2 carrots
2 potatoes
150 g (5 oz) green beans
2 zucchinis (courgettes)
100 g (3½ oz) shelled peas
2 tablespoons chopped flat-leaf parsley

1 Soak the borlotti (pinto)
   beans in plenty of cold water
   overnight. Drain.

2 Heat the oil in a large pan, add
   the onion and cook over low
   heat until soft and translucent.
   Add the garlic and cook for
   1 minute further. Add the pinto
   beans, stock and celery and
   bring to the boil. Reduce
   the heat to low and simmer,
   covered, for 45 minutes, or until
   the beans are almost cooked.

3 Finely chop the carrots, potatoes,
   green beans and zucchinis
   (courgettes) and add to the pan.
   Simmer gently for 15 minutes,
   or until the vegetables are almost
   cooked. Stir in the peas and
   simmer for a further 10 minutes.

4 Season well and stir through the
   chopped parsley.

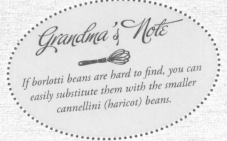

Grandma's Note

*If borlotti beans are hard to find, you can
easily substitute them with the smaller
cannellini (haricot) beans.*

Scones, Cookies & Slices

Cookies are made of butter and love.

Norwegian proverb

Almond Cinnamon Cookies

Preparation time: 12 minutes
Total cooking time: 20 minutes
Makes 45

200 g (6½ oz) blanched almonds
⅓ cup (90 g) caster (berry) sugar
⅓ cup (40 g) icing sugar
3 teaspoons ground cinnamon
¾ cup (90 g) plain (all-purpose) flour
2 egg whites

Vanilla icing
1⅔ cups (210 g) pure icing sugar
1 egg white, lightly beaten
½ teaspoon vanilla essence

1 Preheat the oven to 150°C (300°F/Gas 2). Line a 32 × 28 cm (13 × 11 inch) baking tray with baking paper. Place the almonds, sugars, cinnamon and flour in a food processor. Process for 30 seconds, or until the mixture resembles fine breadcrumbs. Add the egg whites and process for 30 seconds, or until a soft dough forms.

2 Turn the dough onto a lightly floured surface. Knead for 1 minute and shape the dough into a ball. Roll the dough between two sheets of plastic wrap to 5 mm (¼ inch) thickness. Cut into shapes, using a 4 cm (1½ inch) plain or fluted cutter and place on the prepared tray. Bake for 20 minutes, or until lightly golden. Transfer to a wire rack to cool completely.

3 To make the vanilla icing, sift the icing sugar into a small bowl. Make a well in centre and add combined egg white and vanilla essence. Beat the mixture constantly with a wooden spoon until all the icing sugar is incorporated and a firm paste is formed. Using a flat-bladed knife, spread the cookies with icing.

Grandma's Note

You can use 1 teaspoon ground nutmeg instead of cinnamon in the cookies, or spread the cookies with lemon icing instead of vanilla, if preferred. Simply add 2 teaspoons of finely grated lemon rind in place of vanilla essence.

Plain Scones

Preparation time: 20 minutes
Total cooking time: 12 minutes
Makes 12

2 cups (250 g) self-raising flour
pinch salt, optional
30 g (1 oz) butter, cut into small pieces
½ cup (125 ml) milk
⅓ cup (80 ml) water
milk, extra, to glaze
jam (jelly) and whipped cream (topping), to serve

1 Preheat the oven to 210°C (415°F/Gas 6–7). Lightly grease a baking tray. Sift the flour and salt, if using, into a large mixing bowl. Add the butter and rub in lightly using your fingertips.

2 Make a well in the centre of the flour. Add almost all of the combined milk and water. Mix with a flat-bladed knife to a soft dough, adding more liquid if necessary.

3 Turn the dough onto a lightly floured surface (use self-raising flour). Knead the dough briefly and lightly until smooth. Press or roll out the dough to form a round about 1–2 cm (½–¾ inch) thick.

4 Cut the dough into rounds using a floured round 5 cm (2 inch) cutter. Place the rounds on the prepared tray and glaze with the milk. Bake for 10–12 minutes, or until golden brown. Serve with jam (jelly) and whipped cream (topping).

Grandma's Note

Add a pinch of salt to your scones, even the sweet ones. Salt acts as a flavour enhancer and will not be tasted in the cooked product.

Sultana Scones

Preparation time: 20 minutes
Total cooking time: 12 minutes
Makes 12

2 cups (250 g) self-raising flour
pinch salt
30 g (1 oz) butter, cut into small pieces
⅓ cup (90 g) caster (berry) sugar
¼ cup (30 g) sultanas
1 egg, lightly beaten
¾ cup (185 ml) milk
extra milk, to glaze
butter, to serve

1 Preheat the oven to 210°C (415°F/Gas 6–7). Lightly grease a baking tray (sheet). Sift the flour and salt into a large mixing bowl. Add the butter and rub in lightly with fingertips.

2 Add the sugar and sultanas and stir to combine. Make a well in the centre of the mixture. Add the egg and almost all the milk. Mix quickly, with a flat-bladed knife, to a soft dough, adding more milk if necessary. Turn out onto a lightly floured surface and knead briefly until smooth. Press or roll out to form a round about 2 cm (¾ inch) thick.

3 Cut the dough into rounds using a floured plain 5 cm (2 inch) cutter or cut into squares using a floured knife. Place the rounds close together on the prepared tray and brush with extra milk. Bake for 10–12 minutes, or until golden brown. Serve with butter.

Grandma's Tip

Use any type of dried fruit in this recipe, for example, currants, raisins, or chopped and pitted dates or prunes.

Pumpkin Scones

Preparation time: 35 minutes
Total cooking time: 12 minutes
Makes 12

30 g (1 oz) butter, chopped
2 tablespoons caster (berry) sugar
½ cup (125 g) mashed cooked
  pumpkin
1 egg, lightly beaten
½ cup (125 ml) milk
2½ cups (310 g) self-raising flour
pinch salt
milk, to glaze
butter, to serve

1 Preheat the oven to 210°C (415°F/Gas 6–7). Lightly grease a baking tray (sheet). Using electric beaters, beat the butter and sugar in a small mixing bowl until the mixture is light and creamy. Add the pumpkin, egg and milk. Mix until well combined.

2 Sift the flour and salt into a large mixing bowl. Make a well in the centre and add almost all of the mashed pumpkin. Mix lightly, using a flat-bladed knife, to form a soft dough, adding more liquid if necessary.

3 Knead the dough briefly on a lightly floured surface. Roll the dough out to 2 cm (¾ inch) thickness.

4 Cut into rounds using a floured plain 5 cm (2 inch) cutter. Place the rounds, close together, on the prepared tray and brush with a little milk. Bake for 10–12 minutes, or until golden brown. Serve warm with butter.

Grandma's Note

To make ½ cup (125 g) of mashed pumpkin you will need around 250 g (4 oz) of raw pumpkin.

Raspberry Coconut Cookies

Preparation time: 40 minutes
Total cooking time: 10 minutes each tray
Makes 28

60 g butter
½ cup (135 g) caster (berry) sugar
1 egg
⅔ cup (60 g) plain (all-purpose) flour
⅔ cup (60 g) self-raising flour

Icing
100 g packet pink marshmallows
40 g butter
¼ cup (30 g) icing sugar, sifted
½ cup (45 g) desiccated (fine) coconut
⅓ cup (115 g) raspberry jam (jelly)

1 Preheat oven to moderate
   180°C (350°F/Gas 4). Line two oven
   trays (sheets) with baking paper.

2 Using electric beaters, beat the butter
   and sugar in small mixing bowl until
   light and creamy. Transfer to large bowl.
   Add egg; beat until combined. Using a
   metal spoon, fold in sifted flours. Turn
   dough onto lightly floured surface.
   Knead gently for 1 minute or until
   smooth. Roll out dough between baking
   paper to 4 mm thickness. Using a knife
   or fluted pastry wheel, cut dough into
   4.5 × 6 cm (2 × 2½ inch) rectangles.
   Place on prepared trays, allowing room

for spreading. Re-roll remaining pastry
and repeat cutting. Bake for 10 minutes
or until lightly golden. Transfer to wire
rack when cool.

3 To make icing, combine marshmallows
   and butter in small pan. Stir over low
   heat until marshmallows and butter are
   melted and smooth. Stir in icing sugar;
   mix until smooth. Place coconut on
   sheet of greaseproof paper. Working
   quickly, spread about quarter teaspoon
   of icing along each long side of cookie,
   leaving a space in the centre. Dip iced
   cookies into coconut; shake off excess
   coconut.

4 Place jam (jelly) in small pan and heat
   gently until thinned and warm. Spread
   a little jam down centre of each biscuit.

Grandma's Tips

*Cookies can be kept for three days in a
single layer in an airtight container.*

*Stand icing in bowl of hot water while
icing biscuits, to prevent it from
setting too quickly.*

Cherry Slice

Preparation time: 15 minutes
Total cooking time: 35 minutes
Makes about 24

2 cups (250 g) plain (all-purpose) flour
½ cup (60 g) icing sugar
250 g (8 oz) butter, chopped

Topping

30 g (1 oz) butter
⅓ cup (90 g) caster (berry) sugar
1 tablespoon milk
2 teaspoons vanilla essence
¾ cup (90 g) chopped hazelnuts
¾ cup (150 g) sliced red glacé (glazed)
   cherries

1 Preheat the oven to 210°C (415°F/Gas 6–7). Lightly grease an
18 × 28 cm (7 × 11 inch) shallow tin. Line the base with baking
paper, overhanging two opposite sides. Sift the flour and icing
sugar into a mixing bowl. Add the butter and, using your fingertips,
rub in until the mixture forms a dough. Press into prepared tin.
Bake for 15 minutes, or until light golden brown.

2 To make the topping, melt the butter in a small saucepan and add
the sugar, milk and vanilla. Stir, without boiling, until the sugar
dissolves then bring to the boil. Remove from heat. Add the
hazelnuts and cherries to the mixture and stir.

3 Spread the topping over the base. Bake for 15–20 minutes, or until
golden. Cut the slice into squares while still warm and allow to cool
before serving.

Grandma's Tip

Melt dark chocolate
and drizzle over the
cooled slice.

Date and Peach Slice

Preparation time: 15 minutes +
30 minutes soaking
Total cooking time: 40 minutes
Makes 24 pieces

200 g (6½ oz) dried peaches
1 cup (125 g) self-raising flour
1 cup (125 g) plain
    (all-purpose) flour
½ cup (90 g) lightly packed soft
    brown sugar
½ cup (110 g) raw sugar
1½ teaspoons ground cinnamon
¾ cup (45 g) shredded
    (medium) coconut
⅔ cup (125 g) dates, chopped
125 g (4 oz) butter, melted

1 Lightly grease a 23 cm (9 inch) shallow square tin and line with baking paper, overhanging two opposite sides.

2 Roughly chop the peaches and place in a bowl. Cover the peaches with boiling water and leave to soak for 30 minutes. Preheat the oven to 180°C (350°F/Gas 4). Drain the peaches, reserving ½ cup (125 ml) of the liquid.

3 Place the flours, sugars, cinnamon, coconut and dates in a large mixing bowl. Add the melted butter, peaches and reserved liquid and stir gently until only just combined.

4 Spread into the prepared tin and bake for 35–40 minutes, or until golden brown and a skewer inserted into the centre of the slice comes out clean. Cool in the tin for 5 minutes before turning out onto a wire rack to cool completely.

Gingerbread People

Preparation time: 40 minutes +
15 minutes refrigeration
Total cooking time: 10 minutes
Makes 16

125 g (4 oz) unsalted butter, softened
⅓ cup (60 g) lightly packed soft
 brown sugar
¼ cup (90 g) golden (corn) syrup
1 egg, lightly beaten
2 cups (250 g) plain
 (all-purpose) flour
¼ cup (30 g) self-raising flour
1 tablespoon ground ginger
1 teaspoon bicarbonate of soda
 (baking soda)
1 tablespoon currants

Icing
1 egg white
½ teaspoon lemon juice
1¼ cups (155 g) icing sugar, sifted
assorted food colourings

1 Preheat the oven to 180°C
 (350°F/Gas 4). Line two baking
 trays (sheets) with baking paper.

2 Using electric beaters, cream the
 butter, sugar and syrup in a large
 mixing bowl until light and fluffy.
 Add the egg gradually, beating
 well after each addition. Sift the
 dry ingredients over the butter
 mixture and mix with a knife
 until just combined. Combine
 the dough with your hands. Turn
 onto a well-floured surface and
 knead for 1–2 minutes, or until
 smooth. Roll out on a chopping
 board, between two sheets of
 baking paper, to 5 mm (¼ inch)
 thick. Chill on the board for
 15 minutes to firm.

3 Cut the dough into shapes with
 a 13 cm (5 inch) gingerbread
 person cutter. Press the
 remaining dough together and
 re-roll. Cut out shapes and place
 them on the trays. Place the
 currants as eyes and noses. Bake
 for 10 minutes, or until lightly
 browned. Cool on the trays.

4 To make the icing, beat the egg
 white with electric beaters in a
 small, clean, dry bowl until
 foamy. Gradually add the lemon
 juice and icing sugar and beat
 until thick. Divide the icing
 among several bowls and add

the food colourings. Spoon into
small paper icing bags. Seal
ends, snip the tips off the bags
and pipe on faces and clothing.

Grandma's Note

*Store in an airtight container
for up to 3 days.*

Basic Shortbread Fingers

Preparation time: 8 minutes
Total cooking time: 20 minutes
Makes 20 fingers

¾ cup (95 g) cornflour (cornstarch)
⅓ cup (60 g) fine ground rice flour
⅔ cup (85 g) plain (all-purpose) flour
⅓ cup (40 g) icing sugar
200 g unsalted butter, chopped

1   Preheat oven to moderate 180°C
    (350°F/Gas 4). Brush a 32 ×
    28 cm (12½ × 11 inch) baking
    tray (sheet) with melted butter
    or oil, line base with paper;
    grease paper.

2   Sift flours and sugar into large
    mixing bowl; add butter. Using
    fingertips, rub butter into flour
    for 3 minutes or until mixture is
    fine and crumbly. Press mixture
    together with fingers to form a
    soft dough.

3   Press mixture into a shallow
    foil-lined 18 × 27 cm (7 ×
    10½ inch) rectangular tin;
    smooth surface. Turn mixture
    onto a board. Rough up surface
    with a grater or mark with a
    fork if desired. Cut into half

lengthways, then cut each half
into 2 cm (¾ inch) strips.

4   Arrange on prepared tray about
    3 cm (1¼ inch) apart; bake
    20 minutes or until firm and
    lightly golden.

Grandma's Tips

*These shortbreads may be stored in an
airtight container for up to a week.*

Dust with icing sugar to serve.

Passionfruit Shortbread

Preparation time: 45 minutes
Total cooking time: 20 minutes
Makes about 40

250 g (8 oz) butter
⅓ cup (90 g) caster (berry) sugar
2¼ cups (280 g) plain
   (all-purpose) flour
¼ cup (45 g) rice flour
40 g (1¼ oz) white choc melts, melted

Passionfruit icing

1¼ cups (155 g) icing sugar, sifted
2 tablespoons passionfruit pulp
20 g (¾ oz) softened butter
1 tablespoon water

1   Preheat the oven to 160°C (315°F/
    Gas 2–3). Line two baking trays (sheets)
    with baking paper. Using electric beaters,
    beat the butter and caster (berry) sugar
    in a small mixing bowl until light and
    creamy. Fold in the sifted flours and mix
    until a soft dough forms. Turn out onto
    a lightly floured surface. Knead gently
    for 1 minute or until smooth.

2   Roll out the dough between two sheets
    of baking paper 5 mm (¼ inch)
    thickness. Using a sharp knife, cut into
    4 × 4 cm (1½ × 1½ inch) diamonds.
    Place on the prepared trays, allowing
    room for spreading. Re-roll the pastry
    and cut out diamonds in the same way.
    Bake for 15 minutes, or until the
    shortbreads are lightly brown. Stand for
    5 minutes before transferring onto a
    wire rack to cool.

3   To make the passionfruit icing,
    combine the icing sugar, passionfruit
    pulp, butter and water in a bowl to
    form a smooth paste. Stand the bowl
    in pan of simmering water, stirring
    until the icing is smooth and glossy.
    Remove the pan from heat but leave
    the bowl of icing to stand in the warm
    water while icing the shortbreads.
    Using a flat-bladed knife, spread each
    diamond with ½ teaspoon of icing.

4   Leave the biscuits to stand for 15
    minutes to set, then drizzle or pipe a
    decorative pattern on top with the
    melted white chocolate.

Grandma's Notes

These shortbreads can be stored in an airtight
container for up to 2 days.

Overheating the icing will make it dull and
grainy. Try to work as quickly as possible and
dip the knife into hot water occasionally to
give the icing a smooth finish.

Jam Drops

Preparation time: 20 minutes
Total cooking time: 15 minutes
Makes 32

80 g (2¾ oz) unsalted butter, softened
⅓ cup (90 g) caster (berry) sugar
2 tablespoons milk
½ teaspoon vanilla essence
1 cup (125 g) self-raising flour
⅓ cup (40 g) custard powder
⅓ cup (105 g) raspberry jam (jelly)

1 Preheat the oven to 180°C (350°F/Gas 4). Line two baking trays (sheets) with baking paper.

2 Cream the butter and sugar in a small mixing bowl with electric beaters until light and fluffy. Add the milk and vanilla essence and beat until well combined. Add the sifted flour and custard powder and mix to form a soft dough. Roll heaped teaspoons of the mixture into balls and place on the prepared trays.

3 Make an indentation in each ball using the end of a wooden spoon. Fill each hole with a little jam (jelly).

4 Bake for 15 minutes, cool slightly on the trays, then transfer to a wire rack to cool completely.

Choc-Mint Swirls

Preparation time: 30 minutes
Total cooking time: 15 minutes
Makes 22

65 g (2¼ oz) unsalted butter
¼ cup (60 g) caster (berry) sugar
½ cup (60 g) plain (all-purpose) flour
⅓ cup (40 g) self-raising flour
2 tablespoons cocoa powder
1–2 tablespoons milk
22 choc bits

Icing

100 g (3½ oz) unsalted butter, extra
1⅓ cups (165 g) icing sugar
few drops peppermint essence

1 Preheat the oven to 180°C (350°F/Gas 4). Line two 32 × 28 cm (13 × 11 inch) baking trays (sheets) with baking paper. Using electric beaters, beat the butter and sugar in a small mixing bowl until light and creamy. Add the sifted flours, cocoa and milk. Stir with a flat-bladed knife until the mixture forms a soft dough. Turn out onto a piece of baking paper and knead for 1 minute or until smooth.

2 Roll the dough out to 5 mm (¼ inch) thickness. Cut into rounds, using a 4 cm (1½ inch) plain cutter. Place on the prepared tray and bake for 15 minutes. Transfer to a wire rack to cool completely before decorating.

3 To make the filling, beat the butter with electric beaters until soft. Add the icing sugar and beat until smooth, creamy and light. Add the peppermint essence and beat until combined. Using a piping bag fitted with a large fluted nozzle, carefully pipe a flower of peppermint cream onto each cookie. Place a choc bit in the centre of each flower.

Grandma's Notes

Store for up to 2 days in an airtight container.

Dust with one teaspoon each of icing sugar and cocoa powder, sifted together.

Lebkuchen

Preparation time: 25 minutes
Total cooking time: 30 minutes
Makes 35

2⅓ cups (290 g) plain (all-purpose) flour
½ cup (60 g) cornflour (cornstarch)
2 teaspoons cocoa powder
1 teaspoon mixed spice
1 teaspoon ground cinnamon
½ teaspoon ground nutmeg
100 g (3½ oz) unsalted butter, cubed
¾ cup (260 g) golden (corn) syrup
2 tablespoons milk
150 g (5 oz) white chocolate melts
¼ teaspoon mixed spice, extra

1 Preheat the oven to 180°C (350°F/Gas 4). Line two baking trays (sheets) with baking paper.

2 Sift the plain (all-purpose) flour and cornflour (cornstarch), cocoa and spices into a large bowl and make a well in the centre.

3 Place the butter, syrup and milk in a small saucepan, and stir over low heat until butter has melted and mixture is smooth. Remove from the heat and add to the dry ingredients. Mix with a flat-bladed knife until ingredients come together in small beads. Gather together with your hands and turn out onto a sheet of baking paper.

4 Roll the dough out to about 7 mm (⅜ inch) thick. Cut into heart shapes using a 6 cm (2½ inch) cutter. Place on the prepared trays and bake for 25 minutes, or until lightly browned. Cool slightly, then transfer to a wire rack until biscuits are completely cool.

5 Place the chocolate in a heatproof bowl. Bring a saucepan of water to the boil, then remove from heat. Sit the bowl over the pan, making sure the base does not touch the water. Stir until the chocolate has melted.

6 Dip one half of each biscuit into the chocolate and place on a sheet of baking paper until set. Sprinkle with mixed spice.

Raspberry Shortcake

Preparation time: 30 minutes + 50 minutes refrigeration
Total cooking time: 20 minutes
Serves 6–8

1 cup (125 g) plain (all-purpose) flour
4 tablespoons icing sugar
90 g (3 oz) unsalted butter, chilled and cubed
1 egg yolk
½ teaspoon vanilla essence

Topping

750 g (1½ lb) fresh raspberries
3–4 tablespoons icing sugar, to taste
4 tablespoons redcurrant jam (jelly)

1 Put the flour and icing sugar in a food processor. Add the butter and process for 15 seconds, or until the mixture is crumbly. Process for 10 seconds, adding the egg yolk, vanilla essence and enough cold water (about ½–1 tablespoon) to make the dough just come together. Turn out onto a lightly floured surface and gather together into a ball. Wrap in plastic and refrigerate for 30 minutes.

2 Preheat the oven to 180°C (350°F/Gas 4). Roll out the pastry to fit a fluted 20 cm (8 inch) loose-based tart tin and trim the edges. Prick all over with a fork and chill for 20 minutes. Bake for 15–20 minutes, or until golden. Cool on a wire rack.

3 To make the topping, set aside 500 g (1 lb) of the best raspberries and mash the rest with the icing sugar. Spread the mashed raspberries over the shortcake just before serving. Cover with the whole raspberries.

4 Melt the redcurrant jam (jelly) in a small pan until smooth and brush over the raspberries with a soft pastry brush. Serve in slices with thickened (whipping) cream.

Grandma's Tip

You can use 800 g (1 lb 10 oz) frozen raspberries. Thaw in the packet overnight in the fridge and only use when ready to serve.

Vanilla Custard Kisses

Preparation time: 15 minutes
Total cooking time: 12 minutes
Makes 40

125 g (4 oz) unsalted butter
½ cup (125 g) caster (berry) sugar
2 egg yolks
2 teaspoons vanilla essence
⅓ cup (60 g) custard powder
¾ cup (120 g) plain
   (all-purpose) flour
¾ cup (120 g) self-raising flour

Vanilla cream
40 g (1¼ oz) unsalted butter, softened
⅔ cup (110 g) icing sugar
1 teaspoon vanilla essence
1 tablespoon milk

1 Preheat the oven to 180°C (350°F/Gas 4). Grease two 32 × 28 cm (13 × 11 inch) baking trays (sheets) and line with baking paper. Using electric beaters, beat the butter and sugar in a small mixing bowl until mixture is light and creamy. Add the egg yolks one at a time, beating thoroughly after each addition. Add the essence and beat until combined.

2 Transfer the mixture to a large mixing bowl. Using a metal spoon, fold in the sifted custard powder and flours. Stir until ingredients are just combined and the mixture is almost smooth. Press the mixture together with fingertips to form a soft dough.

3 Roll 1 level teaspoon of mixture at a time into balls. Arrange about 5 cm (2 inch) apart on the prepared trays. Flatten lightly with the base of a glass into 2.5 cm (1 inch) rounds. Bake for 12 minutes, or until golden.

4 To make the vanilla cream, beat the butter and essence in a small bowl with a wooden spoon until smooth. Add the sifted icing sugar and milk gradually, stirring until the mixture is smooth.

Leave the cookies on the trays for 5 minutes then transfer to a wire rack to cool. Spread half with the filling and sandwich together with the remaining cookies.

Grandma's Note

Store in an airtight container for up to 2 days.

Anzac Biscuits

Preparation time: 12 minutes
Total cooking time: 20 minutes
Makes 26

1 cup (125 g) plain (all-purpose) flour
⅔ cup (145 g) sugar
1 cup (90 g) rolled oats
1 cup (80 g) desiccated (fine) coconut
125 g unsalted butter
¼ cup (85 g) golden (corn) syrup
½ teaspoon bicarbonate of soda
 (baking soda)
1 tablespoon boiling water

1 Preheat oven to moderate
 180°C (350°F/Gas 4). Line a
 32 × 28 cm (13 × 11 inch)
 baking tray (sheet) with
 baking paper.

2 Sift flour and sugar into large
 mixing bowl. Add oats and
 coconut; make a well in
 the centre.

3 Combine butter and syrup in
 small pan. Stir over low heat
 until butter has melted and
 mixture is smooth; remove from
 heat. Dissolve soda in water; add
 immediately to butter mixture.
 It will foam up instantly.
 Add butter mixture to dry
 ingredients. Using a wooden
 spoon, stir until well combined.

4 Drop one level tablespoon of
 mixture at a time onto prepared
 tray. Flatten gently with fingers,
 allowing room for spreading. Bake
 20 minutes or until just browned.

5 Remove from oven; transfer to
 wire rack to cool.

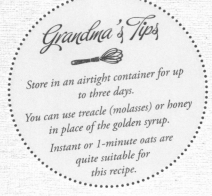

Grandma's Tips

Store in an airtight container for up
to three days.

You can use treacle (molasses) or honey
in place of the golden syrup.

Instant or 1-minute oats are
quite suitable for
this recipe.

Shortbread Stars with Lemon Glaze

Preparation time: 20 minutes
Total cooking time: 15 minutes
Makes 35

2 cups (300 g) plain (all-purpose) flour
2 tablespoons rice flour
200 g unsalted butter
⅓ cup (45 g) icing sugar
1 teaspoon finely grated lemon rind
2 tablespoons lemon juice
silver cachous (sprinkles)

Lemon glaze
1 cup pure icing sugar
2 tablespoons lemon juice, strained
yellow or orange food colouring

1 Preheat oven to moderate 180°C (350°F/Gas 4). Line two 32 × 28 cm (13 × 11 inch) baking trays (sheets) with baking paper.

2 Place flours, butter and sugar in food processor bowl. Using pulse action, press button for 30 seconds or until mixture is fine and crumbly. Add rind and juice; process 20 seconds until mixture forms a dough.

3 Turn out onto a lightly floured surface and knead 20 seconds or until smooth. Roll out to 7 mm thickness; cut out 6 cm star shapes. Bake 15 minutes. Transfer to wire rack to cool.

4 To make lemon glaze, place icing sugar and lemon juice in heatproof bowl over pan of hot water; stir until smooth. Dip cookies face down in glaze, drain excess. Dip toothpick or skewer into food colouring and draw lines into icing before it sets. Decorate centre with silver cachou.

Grandma's Tip

Store up to five days in an airtight container.

Fruity Shortbread Pillows

Preparation time: 1 hour
Total cooking time: 15–20 minutes
Makes 18

2 cups (250 g) plain
   (all-purpose) flour
½ cup (60 g) icing sugar
185 g (6 oz) chilled unsalted
   butter, chopped
1 egg
¼ cup (45 g) fruit mince
1 egg, extra, lightly beaten
icing sugar, to serve

1 Preheat the oven to 180°C (350°F/
   Gas 4). Line two baking trays (sheets)
   with baking paper. Place the flour,
   sugar and butter in a food processor.
   Process for 20 seconds or until the
   mixture resembles fine breadcrumbs.
   Add the egg and process for a further
   15 seconds or until the mixture comes
   together. Turn onto a lightly floured
   surface and knead for 2–3 minutes,
   or until the dough is smooth. Leave the
   dough, covered with plastic wrap, in
   the refrigerator for 10–15 minutes.

2 Divide the pastry in two. Roll half the
   pastry on a sheet of baking paper to
   5 mm (¼ inch) thickness. Lightly mark
   round circles with a 4 cm (1½ inch)
   cutter. Spoon ½ teaspoon of the fruit
   mince into the centre of each circle.
   Brush the pastry with egg.

3 On a sheet of baking paper, roll the
   remaining pastry to 2.5 mm (⅛ inch)
   thickness. (Pastry should be rolled into
   a slightly larger circle, approximately
   1.5 cm (⅝ inch) extra in diameter.)
   Carefully lift the pastry, using the
   rolling pin as a lever, over the top of
   first pastry sheet. Press down between
   the filling to seal the edges. Cut the
   shortbreads, using a floured 4 cm
   (1½ inch) round cutter. (They should
   look like little pillows.) Place on the
   prepared baking trays. Bake for 15–20
   minutes, or until pale golden. Cool on
   trays. Dust liberally with icing sugar
   before serving.

Grandma's Tips

These shortbreads may be stored
in an airtight container for
up to 3 days.

Make different shapes by using
a square or oval cutter,
instead of round.

Coconut Macaroons

Preparation time: 15 minutes
Total cooking time: 15–20 minutes
Makes 60

3 egg whites
1¼ cups (310 g) caster (berry) sugar
½ teaspoon coconut essence
1 teaspoon grated lemon rind
2 tablespoons cornflour
  (cornstarch), sifted
2 cups (180 g) desiccated
  (fine) coconut
125 g (4 oz) dark (semi-sweet)
  chocolate melts, melted

1 Preheat the oven to 180°C (350°F/Gas 4). Line two baking trays (sheets) with baking paper. Place egg whites in a small dry mixing bowl. Using electric beaters, beat the egg whites until firm peaks form. Add the sugar gradually, beating constantly until mixture is thick and glossy and all the sugar is dissolved. Add the coconut essence and rind and beat until just combined.

2 Transfer the mixture to a large mixing bowl and add cornflour (cornstarch) and coconut. Using a metal spoon, stir until just combined.

3 Drop 2 level teaspoons of mixture onto prepared trays about 3 cm (1¼ inch) apart. Bake on the top shelf for 15–20 minutes, or until golden.

4 Leave the macaroons to completely cool on the trays. Dip half of each Macaroon into the melted chocolate and allow to set before serving.

Grandma's Tips

Store in an airtight container
for up to 2 days.

Try sprinkling with shredded (medium)
coconut before baking. Drizzle
with melted chocolate, instead
of dipping, for decoration.

Marzipan Swirls

Preparation time: 20 minutes
Total cooking time: 10–15 minutes
Makes 25

100 g butter
¼ cup (35 g) icing sugar
2 egg yolks
100 g ready-made marzipan, chopped
½ cup (75 g) self-raising flour
½ cup (75 g) plain (all-purpose) flour
coloured cachous (sprinkles),
    for decoration

1 Preheat oven to moderate 180°C (350°F/Gas 4). Line an oven tray (sheet) with baking paper.

2 Using electric beaters, beat butter and icing sugar in a small mixing bowl until light and creamy. Add yolks and beat for another minute. Transfer the mixture to a large mixing bowl.

3 Place the chopped marzipan and the flours in a food processor. Process for 20–30 seconds, or until the mixture resembles fine crumbs. Using a metal spoon, fold the flour mixture into the butter mixture. Stir until smooth. Spoon mixture into a piping bag fitted with a wide, fluted nozzle.

4 Pipe stars about 4 cm (1½ inches) in diameter onto, about 3 cm (1¼ inches) apart to allow room for spreading. Place a cachous (sprinkle) on top of each. Bake 10–15 minutes, or until just golden. Leave on tray for 5 minutes, then transfer to a wire rack to cool. Dust with icing sugar.

Grandma's Notes

Store in an airtight container for up to a week.

Marzipan log is readily available in most supermarkets and some delicatessens.

Gingernuts

Preparation time: 15 minutes
Total cooking time: 15 minutes
Makes 50

2 cups (250 g) plain
    (all-purpose) flour
½ teaspoon bicarbonate of soda
    (baking soda)
1 tablespoon ground ginger
½ teaspoon mixed spice
125 g (4 oz) unsalted butter, chopped
1 cup (185 g) lightly packed soft
    brown sugar
¼ cup (60 ml) boiling water
1 tablespoon golden (corn) syrup

1   Preheat the oven to 180°C (350°F/Gas 4). Line two baking trays (sheets) with baking paper.

2   Sift the flour, bicarbonate of soda (baking soda), ginger and mixed spice into a large mixing bowl. Add the butter and sugar and rub into the flour with your fingertips until the mixture resembles fine breadcrumbs.

3   Pour the boiling water into a small heatproof jug, add the syrup and stir until dissolved. Add to the flour mixture and mix to a soft dough with a flat-bladed knife.

4   Roll into balls using 2 heaped teaspoons of mixture at a time. Place on the prepared trays, allowing room for spreading, and flatten out slightly with your fingertips. Bake for 15 minutes, or until well-coloured and firm. Leave to cool on the trays for 10 minutes before transferring to a wire rack to cool completely. Repeat with the remaining mixture.

Grandma's Tips

Store in an airtight container for up to 5 days.

If you want to dress the gingernuts up, make icing by combining 2–3 teaspoons lemon juice, ½ cup (60 g) sifted icing sugar and 10 g (¼ oz) melted butter in a bowl. Mix until smooth, then spread over the top and allow to set.

Chocolate Chip Cookies

Preparation time: 10 minutes
Total cooking time: 15 minutes
Makes 24

150 g unsalted butter
¼ cup (55 g) soft brown sugar
⅓ cup (75 g) caster (berry) sugar
1 egg yolk
1 teaspoon vanilla essence
1½ cups (225 g) self-raising flour
1 cup (200 g) choc dots

1   Preheat oven to moderate
    180°C (350°F/Gas 4). Line a
    32 × 28 cm (13 × 11 inch)
    baking tray (sheet) with
    baking paper.

2   Using electric beaters, beat
    butter, sugars and yolk in small
    mixing bowl until light and
    creamy. Add essence, beat
    until combined.

3   Transfer mixture to large mixing
    bowl; add flour and two-thirds
    of the choc dots. Using a metal
    spoon, stir until ingredients are
    just combined.

4   Using fingers, press mixture
    together to form a soft dough.
    Roll one tablespoon of mixture
    at a time into a ball.

5   Press remaining choc dots firmly
    on top of balls. Arrange on
    prepared tray, allowing room for
    spreading. Bake 15 minutes or
    until crisp and lightly browned.
    Cool cookies on trays.

Grandma's Tips

Store in an airtight container for
up to three days.

Instead of choc dots, you can
use half chopped white chocolate
and any selection of
chopped nuts.

Moist Chocolate Brownies

Preparation time: 20 minutes
Total cooking time: 45 minutes
Makes 36 squares

1½ cups (225 g) plain (all-purpose) flour
¼ cup (30 g) cocoa powder
1 teaspoon baking powder
½ teaspoon bicarbonate of soda
   (baking soda)
½ cup (60 g) chopped macadamia nuts
125 g unsalted butter
200 g (7 oz) dark (semi-sweet) cooking
   chocolate, chopped
1 cup caster (berry) sugar
2 eggs, lightly beaten
⅓ cup (80 g) sour cream
⅓ cup (40 g) chopped macadamia nuts, extra

Chocolate cream topping
150 g (5½ oz) dark (semi-sweet) cooking
   chocolate, chopped
½ cup (125 g) sour cream

1 Preheat oven to moderate 180°C
   (350°F/Gas 4). Brush a shallow, 23 cm
   (9 inch) square cake tin with melted
   butter or oil. Line base and sides with
   paper; grease paper.

2 Sift flour with other dry ingredients
   into large mixing bowl; add nuts.
   Make a well in centre.

3 Place butter and chocolate in medium
   heatproof bowl. Stand over pan of
   simmering water and stir until chocolate
   is melted and mixture is smooth.
   Remove from heat; add sugar, eggs and
   cream. Beat with a wire whisk until
   ingredients are well combined and

mixture is thick and smooth. Add
chocolate mixture to dry ingredients.
Using a wooden spoon, stir until well
combined; do not overbeat. Spread
mixture into prepared tin. Bake
40 minutes or until skewer comes out
clean when inserted in centre of slice.
Cool in tin.

4 To make chocolate cream topping,
   place chocolate in medium heatproof
   bowl. Stand over pan of simmering
   water and stir until chocolate is melted.
   Remove from heat; stand 2 minutes.
   Add cream and beat with a wire whisk
   until mixture is thick and glossy. While
   still warm, spread the topping over the
   slice and sprinkle with nuts; allow
   to set before cutting into 4 cm
   (1½ inch) squares.

Grandma's Tips

*Brownies may be stored in an
airtight container for up
to two days.*

*You can use pecans or
walnuts in place of
macadamia nuts.*

Walnut Brownies

Preparation time: 10 minutes
Total cooking time: 35 minutes
Makes 20 diamonds

100 g (3½ oz) unsalted butter
⅔ cup (125 g) lightly packed soft
  brown sugar
¼ cup (40 g) sultanas, chopped
¾ cup (185 ml) water
1 cup (125 g) self-raising flour
1 cup (125 g) plain (all-purpose) flour
1 teaspoon ground cinnamon
1 tablespoon cocoa powder
½ cup (60 g) chopped walnuts
¼ cup (90 g) choc bits
20 walnut halves

Icing

60 g (2 oz) unsalted butter
¾ cup (90 g) icing sugar
1 tablespoon cocoa powder
1 tablespoon milk

1 Preheat the oven to 180°C (350°F/Gas 4). Lightly grease a 27 × 18 cm (11 × 7 inch) shallow rectangular tin. Line the base with baking paper, extending it over the two longer sides. Grease the paper. Combine the butter, sugar, sultanas and water in a small saucepan. Constantly stir over low heat for 5 minutes, or until the butter is melted and the sugar dissolved. Remove from the heat.

2 Sift the dry ingredients into a large mixing bowl and add the nuts and choc bits. Make a well in the centre of the dry ingredients and add the butter mixture. Using a wooden spoon, stir until just combined. Do not overmix.

3 Spoon the mixture evenly into the prepared tin and smooth the surface. Bake for 30 minutes, or until a skewer comes out clean when inserted in the centre of the slice. Leave in the tin for 20 minutes before turning onto a wire rack to cool.

4 To make the icing, beat the butter with electric beaters until light and creamy. Add the sugar, cocoa powder and milk. Beat until smooth. Spread the icing over the brownie. Cut into diamonds and top with walnuts.

Chocolate Caramel Slice

Preparation time: 15 minutes + refrigeration
Total cooking time: 20 minutes
Makes 24 triangles

125 g (4 oz) plain sweet wheatmeal (digestive) biscuits, crushed
80 g (2¾ oz) unsalted butter, melted
2 tablespoons desiccated (fine) coconut
400 g (13 oz) can sweetened condensed milk
125 g (4 oz) butter
⅓ cup (90 g) caster (berry) sugar
⅓ cup (115 g) golden (corn) syrup
250 g (8 oz) milk chocolate melts
1 tablespoon vegetable oil

1 Lightly grease a shallow 30 × 20 cm (12 × 8 inch) rectangular cake tin and line with aluminium foil. Grease the foil. Combine the biscuits, melted butter and coconut together in a medium mixing bowl. Press the mixture evenly into the prepared tin and smooth the surface.

2 Combine the condensed milk, butter, sugar and syrup in a small pan. Stir over low heat for 15 minutes or until the sugar has dissolved and the mixture is smooth, thick and lightly browned. Remove from heat and leave to cool slightly. Pour over the biscuit base and smooth the surface.

3 Place the milk chocolate melts and oil in a small heatproof bowl. Stand over a pan of simmering water, stir until melted. Spread the chocolate mixture over caramel. Allow to partially set before marking into 24 triangles. Refrigerate until firm.

Grandma's Tips

Slice may be stored in an airtight container for up to 2 days.

You can use dark chocolate melts in place of milk chocolate.

Chocolate Carrot Slice

Preparation time: 15 minutes
Total cooking time: 30 minutes
Makes 32

1 cup (150 g) self-raising flour
1 teaspoon ground cinnamon
¾ cup (170 g) caster (berry) sugar
½ cup (70 g) finely grated carrot
1 cup mixed dried fruit
½ cup (180 g) choc bits
⅓ cup (25 g) desiccated (fine) coconut
2 eggs, lightly beaten
90 g (3 oz) unsalted butter, melted
⅓ cup (40 g) chopped walnuts

Cream cheese frosting
125 g (4½ oz) cream cheese
30 g (1 oz) unsalted butter
1½ cups (210 g) icing sugar, sifted
1 teaspoon hot water

1 Preheat oven to moderate 180°C (350°F/Gas 4). Brush a shallow 23 cm (9 inch) square cake tin with melted butter or oil and line the base and sides with baking paper.

2 Sift flour and cinnamon into a large mixing bowl. Add caster (berry) sugar, grated carrot, mixed fruit, choc bits and coconut and stir until just combined. Add beaten eggs and butter. Stir until the mixture is just combined.

3 Spread mixture evenly into prepared tin and smooth surface. Bake for 30 minutes or until golden. Cool in tin, turn out.

4 To make cream cheese frosting, use electric beaters. Beat cream cheese and butter in small mixing bowl until smooth. Add icing sugar and beat for 2 minutes or until mixture is light and fluffy. Add water; beat until combined. Spread slice with frosting using a flat-bladed knife and sprinkle with walnuts. Cut into 16 squares, then cut each square into triangles.

Grandma's Tips

Store for up to two days in an airtight container or up to two months in the freezer, without icing.
This slice is also delicious without icing.

Pastries & Tarts

I don't think a really good pie can be made
without a dozen or so children peeking over your shoulder
as you stoop to look in at it every little while.

John Gould

Apple Pie

*Preparation time: 45 minutes +
  cooling time*
Total cooking time: 50 minutes
Serves 6

6 large Granny Smith apples, peeled,
  cored and cut into wedges
2 tablespoons caster (berry) sugar
1 teaspoon finely grated lemon rind
pinch of ground cloves
2 tablespoons apricot jam (jelly)
1 egg, lightly beaten
1 tablespoon sugar

Pastry
2 cups (250 g) plain (all-purpose) flour
3 tablespoons self-raising flour
150 g (5 oz) butter, chilled and cubed
2 tablespoons caster (berry) sugar
4–5 tablespoons iced water

1 Put the apples in a large
   heavy-based pan with the
   sugar, lemon rind, cloves and
   2 tablespoons water. Cover and
   simmer for 8 minutes, or until
   just tender, shaking the pan
   occasionally. Drain and cool.

2 To make the pastry, sift the
   flours into a bowl. Rub the
   butter into the flour with your
   fingertips until the mixture
   resembles fine breadcrumbs. Add
   the sugar, mix well and make a
   well in the centre. Add the water
   and mix with a flat-bladed knife,
   using a cutting action, until the
   mixture comes together in beads.
   Gather the pastry together on a
   floured surface. Divide into two,
   making one half a little bigger.
   Wrap in plastic and refrigerate
   for 20 minutes.

3 Preheat the oven to 200°C
   (400°F/Gas 6). Roll out the
   larger piece of pastry between
   two sheets of baking paper to
   line a 23 cm (9 inch) pie plate,
   trimming away the excess pastry.
   Brush the jam (jelly) over the base
   and spoon in the apple filling.
   Roll out the remaining piece of
   pastry between the baking paper
   until large enough to cover the
   pie. Brush a little water around
   the rim, to secure the top. Trim
   off the excess pastry, pinch the
   edges together and cut steam
   slits in the top.

4 Roll out the trimmings to make
   leaves to decorate the pie top.
   Brush the top lightly with egg
   and sprinkle with sugar. Bake
   for 20 minutes, then reduce the
   oven to 180°C (350°F/Gas 4)
   and bake for 15–20 minutes, or
   until golden.

Bramble Pie

Preparation time: 30 minutes +
  30 minutes refrigeration
Total cooking time: 40 minutes
Serves 4–6

1 cup (125 g) self-raising flour
1 cup (125 g) plain (all-purpose) flour
125 g (4 oz) unsalted butter, chilled
  and cubed
2 tablespoons caster (berry) sugar
1 egg, lightly beaten
3–4 tablespoons milk

Filling
2 tablespoons cornflour (cornstarch)
2–4 tablespoons caster (berry) sugar,
  to taste
1 teaspoon grated orange rind
1 tablespoon orange juice
600 g (1¼ lb) brambles
1 egg yolk, mixed with 1 teaspoon
  water, to glaze

1 Mix the flours, butter and
sugar in a food processor for
30 seconds or until the mixture
is fine and crumbly. Add the egg
and almost all the milk; process
for another 15 seconds or until
the mixture comes together,
adding more milk if needed.
Turn onto a lightly floured
surface and gather into a ball.
Refrigerate for 30 minutes.

2 To make the filling, put the
cornflour (cornstarch); caster
(berry) sugar, orange rind and
juice in a pan and mix well. Add
half the brambles and stir over
low heat for 5 minutes or until
the mixture boils and thickens.
Leave to cool, then add the
remaining brambles. Pour into
a 750 ml (24 fl oz) pie dish.

3 Preheat the oven to 180°C
(350°F/Gas 4). Divide the
pastry dough in half and roll out
one half until large enough to
cover the dish, trimming away
the excess. Roll out the other
half and, using heart-shaped
pastry cutters of various sizes, cut
out enough hearts to cover the
pie top. Brush the pie top with
egg glaze. Bake for 35 minutes
or until golden brown.

Grandma's Note

Brambles include any creeping
stem berries, such as boysenberries,
blackberries, loganberries and
youngberries. Use just one variety or a
combination. You could use frozen or
canned berries if you drain
them well.

Pear and Pecan Pie

Preparation time: 25 minutes +
  40 minutes refrigeration + cooling
Total cooking time: 50 minutes
Serves 6

Pastry

1½cups (185 g) plain (all-purpose) flour
75 g (2½ oz) unsalted butter, chilled and
  cubed
50 g (1½ oz) Copha (white vegetable
  shortening), chilled and cubed
1 teaspoon caster (berry) sugar
2–3 tablespoons iced water

Filling

40 g (1¼ oz) unsalted butter
½ cup (180 g) golden (corn) syrup
2 tablespoons cornflour (cornstarch)
¼ teaspoon ground ginger
½ teaspoon grated lemon rind
½ teaspoon mixed spice
4 pears, peeled, cored and thinly sliced
1 cup (100 g) pecans, chopped
1 tablespoon caster (berry) sugar
1 tablespoon ground pecans
1 tablespoon sugar
1 egg, lightly beaten

1 To make the pastry, sift the flour and
   ¼ teaspoon salt into a large bowl and
   rub in the butter and Copha (white
   vegetable shortening) with your
   fingertips until the mixture resembles
   fine breadcrumbs. Mix in the sugar.
   Make a well, add almost all the water
   and mix with a flat-bladed knife, using
   a cutting action, until the mixture
   comes together in beads, adding more
   water if necessary.

2 Gather the dough together and lift
   onto a lightly floured work surface.
   Press into a ball and flatten slightly

into a disc. Cover in plastic wrap and
refrigerate for 20 minutes.

3 Preheat the oven to 200°C (400°F/
   Gas 6) and heat a baking tray (sheet).
   Grease an 18 cm (7 inch) pie dish.
   Roll out two-thirds of the pastry
   between two sheets of baking paper to
   line the dish, trimming away the
   excess. Cover and refrigerate for
   20 minutes.

4 For the filling, heat the butter and
   syrup in a saucepan over medium heat
   for 2 minutes. Add the cornflour
   (cornstarch), ginger, rind and mixed
   spice and stir until smooth. Add the
   pears, then stir in half the chopped
   pecans and cook for 5 minutes, or until
   the pear is tender. Cool completely.

5 Combine the caster (berry) sugar and
   remaining chopped pecans and scatter
   over the pastry base. Add the filling.

6 Combine the ground pecans and sugar.
   Roll out the remaining pastry to form a
   pie lid. Brush with beaten egg. Cut long
   wide strips of paper and arrange over
   the pie lid in straight lines with wide
   gaps between. Scatter the nut and sugar
   mixture over the exposed pastry and roll
   lightly with the rolling pin to embed
   them. Lift off the paper strips, then
   position the lid on the pie, pinching the
   edges down to seal. Trim the rim.

7 Bake on the hot tray in the centre of
   the oven for 20 minutes. Reduce the
   oven to 180°C (350°F/Gas 4), cover
   the top with foil and bake for another
   20 minutes. Cool in the tin. Serve
   warm or cold.

Cherry Pie

Preparation time: 25 minutes +
*   15 minutes refrigeration*
Total cooking time: 40 minutes
Serves 6–8

1¼ cups (155 g) plain
    (all-purpose) flour
¼ cup (30 g) icing sugar
60 g (2 oz) ground almonds
100 g (3½ oz) unsalted butter, chilled
    and cubed
3 tablespoons iced water
2 × 700 g (1 lb 6 oz) jars pitted
    morello cherries, drained
1 egg, lightly beaten
caster (berry) sugar, to sprinkle

1 Sift the flour and icing sugar into a bowl and then stir in the ground almonds. Add the butter and rub in with your fingertips until the mixture resembles fine breadcrumbs. Add almost all the water and cut into the flour mixture with a knife until the mixture forms beads, adding the remaining water if necessary.

2 Turn the dough out onto a lightly floured surface and press together until smooth. Roll out the dough to a circle about 25 cm (10 inches). Cover with plastic wrap and refrigerate for about 15 minutes.

3 Preheat the oven to 200°C (400°F/Gas 6). Spoon the cherries into a 23 cm (9 inch) round pie dish. Cover the pie dish with the pastry top and trim away the excess. Roll out the trimmings to make decorations. Brush the pastry top with beaten egg to secure the decorations on top. Sprinkle lightly with caster (berry) sugar. Place the pie dish on a baking tray to catch drips and cook for 35–40 minutes or until golden.

Pecan Pie

Preparation time: 30 minutes +
 chilling
Total cooking time: 1 hour
 15 minutes
Serves 6

1½ cups (185 g) plain
 (all-purpose) flour
100 g (3½ oz) cold butter, chopped
2 tablespoons iced water

Filling

2 cups (200 g) whole pecans
 3 eggs
60 g (2¼ oz) butter, melted
⅔ cup (155 g) soft brown sugar
⅔ cup (170 ml) golden (corn) syrup
1 teaspoon vanilla essence

1 Sift the flour into a bowl then
   rub in the butter with your
   fingertips. Add the water and
   mix it in with a flat-bladed
   knife, using a cutting action,
   until the mixture comes together
   in beads. Gather the dough
   together, cover with plastic wrap
   and refrigerate for 20 minutes.

2 Transfer the dough to a sheet of
   baking paper and roll it out to
   a 3 mm (⅛ inch) thickness. It
   should be large enough to line
   a 23 cm (9 inch) pie dish, with
   some left over to decorate the
   edge. Invert the pastry into the
   dish and remove the baking
   paper. Line the dish with the
   pastry, and remove the excess.
   Gather the dough scraps together
   and roll them out to a 3 mm
   (⅛ inch) thickness. Using small
   cutters, cut shapes from the
   pastry. Brush the pastry rim with

water, and attach the pastry
shapes. Refrigerate for
20 minutes. Preheat the oven
to 180°C (350°F/Gas 4).

3 Cover the edge of the pastry
   with strips of foil to prevent
   burning. Line the pastry shell
   with a sheet of crumpled baking
   paper, and fill with baking
   beads. Bake for 15 minutes,
   then remove the beads and

paper and bake for 15 minutes
more, until the base is lightly
golden. Remove the foil and
cool before filling.

4 Place the pecans on the pastry
   base. Whisk together the eggs,
   butter, sugar, syrup, vanilla and
   a good pinch of salt. Pour over
   the pecans. Place the pie dish
   on a baking tray, and bake for
   45 minutes. Cool completely.

Lemon Meringue Pie

Preparation time: 30 minutes +
* 20 minutes refrigeration*
Total cooking time: 50 minutes
Serves 4–6

375 g (12 oz) sweet shortcrust pastry
¼ cup (30 g) plain (all-purpose) flour
¼ cup (30 g) cornflour (cornstarch)
1 cup (250 g) caster (berry) sugar
¾ cup (185 ml) lemon juice
1 tablespoon grated lemon rind
50 g (1½ oz) unsalted
    butter, chopped
6 egg yolks

Meringue
6 egg whites
1⅓ cups (340 g) caster (berry) sugar
pinch of cream of tartar

1   Lightly grease an 18 cm (7 inch)
    pie plate. Roll out the pastry
    between two sheets of baking
    paper into a 30 cm (12 inch)
    circle to line the pie plate,
    trimming away the excess.

2   Re-roll the pastry trimmings
    and cut into three 10 × 2 cm
    (4 × ¾ inch) strips. Brush the
    pie rim with water, place the
    pastry strips around the top of
    the pastry rim and use your
    fingers to make a decorative
    edge. Prick all over the base with
    a fork. Cover and refrigerate for
    20 minutes. Preheat the oven
    to 180°C (350°F/Gas 4).

3   Line the pastry with baking
    paper and spread with a layer of
    baking beads or rice. Bake for
    15 minutes, then remove the
    paper and beads and bake for
    15–20 minutes, or until dry.
    Leave to cool. Increase the oven
    to 200°C (400°F/Gas 6).

4   To make the lemon filling, put
    the flours, sugar, lemon juice
    and rind in a saucepan.
    Gradually add 1¼ cups (315 ml)
    water and whisk over medium

heat until smooth. Cook,
stirring, for another 2 minutes,
or until thickened. Remove
from the heat and vigorously
whisk in the butter and egg
yolks. Return to low heat and
stir for 2 minutes, or until
very thick.

5   To make the meringue, beat the
    egg whites, sugar and cream of
    tartar in a clean, dry bowl with
    electric beaters, for 10 minutes
    until thick and glossy.

6   Spread the lemon filling into the
    cooled pastry base, then spread
    the meringue over the top,
    piling high in the centre and
    forming into peaks with a knife.
    Bake for 8–10 minutes, or until
    lightly browned.

Plum Pie

Preparation time: 15 minutes +
20 minutes refrigeration
Total cooking time: 55 minutes
Serves 8

600 g (1¼ lb) sweet shortcrust pastry
14 large plums, halved, stoned and
    roughly chopped, or 2 × 825 g
    (1 lb 11 oz) tins plums, drained
½ cup (90 g) soft brown sugar
1 teaspoon grated lemon rind
1 teaspoon grated orange rind
30 g (1 oz) unsalted butter, softened
2 tablespoons plain (all-purpose) flour

½ teaspoon ground cinnamon
1 egg, lightly beaten
caster (berry) sugar, for sprinkling

1 Preheat the oven to 180°C
   (350°F/Gas 4). Grease a 23 cm
   (9 inch) pie tin.

2 Roll out two-thirds of the pastry
   between two sheets of baking
   paper to line the tin, trimming
   away the excess pastry.
   Refrigerate with the remaining
   pastry for 20 minutes.

3 Combine the plums, brown
   sugar, citrus rind and butter in a
   large bowl. Sift the flour and
   cinnamon together over the
   plums and fold through. Place
   in the pie tin. Roll out the
   remaining pastry to cover the tin
   and trim the edge. Pinch the
   edges and make a small steam
   hole in the centre. Brush with
   egg and bake for 55 minutes,
   or until the pastry is golden.
   Sprinkle with caster (berry)
   sugar before serving.

Rhubarb Pie

Preparation time: 40 minutes +
  30 minutes refrigeration + cooling
Total cooking time: 1 hour
Serves 6

2 cups (250 g) plain
  (all-purpose) flour
30 g (1 oz) unsalted butter, chilled
  and cubed
70 g (2¼ oz) Copha (white vegetable
  shortening), chilled and cubed
2 tablespoons icing sugar
150 ml (5 fl oz) iced water

Filling

1.5 kg (3 lb) rhubarb, trimmed
  and chopped
1 cup (250 g) caster (berry) sugar
½ teaspoon ground cinnamon
2½ tablespoons cornflour (cornstarch)
30 g (1 oz) unsalted butter, cubed
1 egg, lightly beaten
icing sugar, to dust

1 Grease a 20 cm (8 inch) ceramic pie
  dish. Sift the flour and ½ teaspoon salt
  into a large bowl and rub in the butter
  and Copha (white vegetable shortening)
  with your fingertips until the mixture
  resembles fine breadcrumbs. Stir in the
  icing sugar. Make a well, add almost all
  the water and mix with a flat-bladed
  knife, using a cutting action, until it
  comes together in beads. Add more
  water if necessary.

2 Gently gather the dough together and
  lift onto a lightly floured work surface.
  Press into a ball, flatten into a disc,
  wrap in plastic and refrigerate for
  30 minutes.

3 Put the rhubarb, sugar, cinnamon and
  2 tablespoons water in a saucepan and
  stir over low heat until the sugar is
  dissolved. Simmer, covered, for 5–8
  minutes, stirring occasionally, until the
  rhubarb is tender. Mix the cornflour
  (cornstarch) with ¼ cup (60 ml) water
  and add to the pan. Bring to the boil,
  stirring until thickened. Allow to cool.
  Preheat the oven to 180°C (350°F/
  Gas 4) and heat a baking tray (sheet).

4 Roll out two-thirds of the dough to a
  30 cm (12 inch) circle to line the pie
  dish. Spoon the rhubarb into the dish.
  Dot with butter.

5 Roll out the remaining pastry to form
  a lid. Moisten the pie rim with egg and
  press the top in place. Trim the edges
  and make a slit in the top. Decorate
  with pastry trimmings. Brush with egg
  and bake on the hot tray for 35–40
  minutes, or until golden. Dust with
  icing sugar to serve.

Summer Berry Tart

Preparation time: 35 minutes +
20 minutes refrigeration
Total cooking time: 35 minutes
Serves 4–6

1 cup (125 g) plain (all-purpose) flour
90 g (3 oz) unsalted butter, chilled
 and cubed
2 tablespoons icing sugar
1–2 tablespoons iced water

Filling

3 egg yolks
2 tablespoons caster (berry) sugar
2 tablespoons cornflour (cornstarch)
1 cup (250 ml) milk
1 teaspoon vanilla essence
250 g (8 oz) strawberries, halved
125 g (4 oz) blueberries
125 g (4 oz) raspberries
1–2 tablespoons redcurrant
 jam (jelly)

1 Preheat the oven to 180°C
 (350°F/Gas 4). Mix the flour,
 butter and icing sugar in a food
 processor for 15 seconds or until
 fine and crumbly. Add enough
 of the water to make the dough
 just come together. Turn out
 onto a lightly floured surface
 and press together into a ball.
 Roll out to line a 20 cm (8 inch)
 fluted tart tin, trimming away
 the excess. Refrigerate for
 20 minutes. Line with baking
 paper and spread with a layer of
 baking beads or rice. Bake for
 15 minutes, then remove the
 paper and beads. Bake for
 another 15 minutes, or until the
 pastry is dry and lightly golden.

2 Whisk the egg yolks, sugar and
 cornflour (cornstarch) until
 pale. Heat the milk in a small
 pan until almost boiling, then
 add gradually to the egg
 mixture, beating constantly.
 Strain into the pan. Stir over low
 heat for 3 minutes or until the
 custard boils and thickens.
 Remove from the heat and add
 the vanilla. Transfer to a bowl,
 lay plastic wrap directly on the
 surface to prevent a skin
 forming, and leave to cool.

3 Spread the custard in the pastry
 shell. Top with the strawberries,
 blueberries and raspberries. Heat
 the redcurrant jam (jelly) until
 liquid in a small pan or in the
 microwave and brush over the
 fruit with a soft pastry brush.

Pear and Almond Flan

*Preparation time: 15 minutes +
    2 hours 30 minutes chilling
Total cooking time: 1 hour
    10 minutes
Serves 8*

1¼ cups (155 g) plain
    (all-purpose) flour
90 g (3 oz) butter, chilled and cubed
¼ cup (60 g) caster (berry) sugar
2 egg yolks
1 tablespoon iced water

Filling

165 g (5½ oz) butter, softened
⅔ cup (160 g) caster (berry) sugar
3 eggs
1¼ cups (230 g) ground almonds
1½ tablespoons plain
    (all-purpose) flour
2 ripe pears

1 Grease a shallow 24 cm (9½ inch) loose-based tart tin. Place the flour, butter and sugar in a food processor and process until the mixture resembles breadcrumbs. Add the egg yolks and water and mix until the dough just comes together. Turn out onto a lightly floured surface and gather into a ball. Wrap in plastic and refrigerate for 30 minutes. Preheat the oven to 180°C (350°F/Gas 4).

2 Roll the pastry between two sheets of baking paper until large enough to line the tin, trimming off any excess. Sparsely prick the base with a fork. Line with baking paper, spread with a layer of baking beads or rice and bake for 10 minutes. Remove the paper and beads and bake for 10 minutes.

3 To make the filling, mix the butter and sugar with electric beaters for 30 seconds (don't cream the mixture). Add the eggs one at a time, beating after each addition. Fold in the ground almonds and flour and spread smoothly over the cooled pastry base.

4 Peel and halve the pears lengthways and remove the cores. Cut the pears crossways into 3 mm (⅛ inch) slices. Separate the slices slightly, then place each half on top of the tart to form a cross. Bake for about 50 minutes, or until the filling has set (the middle may still be a little soft). Cool in the tin, then refrigerate for at least 2 hours before serving.

Blackberry Pie

Preparation time: 20 minutes +
30 minutes refrigeration
Total cooking time: 40 minutes
Serves 6

500 g (1 lb) sweet shortcrust pastry
500 g (1 lb) blackberries
⅔ cup (160 g) caster (berry) sugar
2 tablespoons cornflour (cornstarch)
milk, to brush
1 egg, lightly beaten
caster (berry) sugar, extra,
    to sprinkle

1 Preheat the oven to 200°C (400°F/Gas 6). Grease a 20 cm (8 inch) pie dish. Roll out two-thirds of the pastry between two sheets of baking paper until large enough to line the dish, pressing firmly into place and trimming away the excess.

2 Toss the blackberries, sugar and cornflour (cornstarch) together in a bowl until well mixed, then transfer to the pie dish. Roll out the remaining pastry between two sheets of baking paper until large enough to cover the pie. Moisten the rim of the pie base with milk and press the pastry lid firmly into place. Trim and crimp the edges. Brush with egg and sprinkle with the extra sugar. Pierce the top of the pie with a knife.

3 Bake on the bottom shelf of the oven for 10 minutes. Reduce the oven to 180°C (350°F/Gas 4) and move the pie to the centre. Bake for another 30 minutes, or until golden on top. Cool before serving.

Banoffie Pie

Preparation time: 35 minutes +
* 50 minutes refrigeration*
Total cooking time: 40 minutes
Serves 8

1¼ cups (150 g) plain (all-purpose) flour
2 tablespoons icing sugar
90 g (3 oz) ground walnuts
80 g (2¾ oz) unsalted butter, chilled
  and cubed
2–3 tablespoons iced water

Filling
400 g (13 oz) condensed milk
30 g (1 oz) unsalted butter
1 tablespoon golden (corn) syrup
4 bananas, sliced
1½ cups (375 ml) thickened
  (whipping) cream
50 g (1¾ oz) dark (semi-sweet)
  chocolate, melted

1 Sift the flour and icing sugar into a large bowl. Add the walnuts. Rub in the butter until the mixture resembles fine breadcrumbs. Add the water, mixing with a knife until the dough just comes together. Turn out onto a lightly floured surface and press together into a ball. Wrap in plastic and refrigerate for 15 minutes. Roll out until large enough to line a 23 cm (9 inch) tart tin, trimming away the excess. Refrigerate for 20 minutes.

2 Preheat the oven to 180°C (350°F/Gas 4). Cover the pastry with baking paper and spread with a layer of baking beads or rice. Bake for 15 minutes, then remove the paper and beads. Bake the pastry for another 20 minutes, or until dry and lightly golden. Leave to cool completely.

3 Heat the condensed milk, butter and syrup in a small pan for 5 minutes, stirring constantly until it boils, thickens and turns light caramel. Cool slightly. Arrange half the banana over the pastry and pour the caramel over the top. Refrigerate for 30 minutes.

4 Whip the cream and spoon over the caramel. Top with more banana and drizzle with melted chocolate.

Prune and Almond Custard Tart

Preparation time: 2 hours + 1 hour
   soaking + refrigeration
Total cooking time: 50 minutes
Serves 6–8

375 g (12 oz) pitted prunes
⅔ cup (170 ml) muscat or sweet sherry
4 tablespoons redcurrant jam (jelly)

Almond shortcrust pastry
1½ cups (185 g) plain (all-purpose) flour
⅓ cup (60 g) ground almonds
¼ cup (60 g) caster (berry) sugar
125 g (4 oz) unsalted butter, chilled and cubed
1 egg yolk
2–3 tablespoons iced water
60 g (2 oz) marzipan, grated

Custard cream
3 tablespoons custard powder
1⅔ cups (410 ml) milk
½ cup (125 g) sour cream
1 tablespoon caster (berry) sugar
2 teaspoons vanilla essence

1 Put the prunes in a pan with the muscat or sherry, leave to soak for 1 hour, then simmer over very low heat for 10 minutes, or until the prunes are tender but not mushy. Remove from the liquid with a slotted spoon and leave to cool. Add the redcurrant jam (jelly) to the pan and stir over low heat until dissolved. Cover and set aside.

2 To make the pastry, mix the flour, almonds and sugar in a food processor for 15 seconds. Add the butter and process for 15 seconds until crumbly. Add the egg yolk and enough water to make the dough just come together. Turn out

onto a lightly floured surface and gather into a ball. Refrigerate for 15 minutes. Preheat the oven to 180°C (350°F/Gas 4) and heat a baking tray (sheet).

3 Roll out the pastry between two sheets of baking paper until large enough to line a lightly greased 23 cm (9 inch) loose-based tart tin, trimming away the excess. (If it is still too soft, the pastry may need to be refrigerated for another 10 minutes.)

4 Cover the pastry with baking paper and spread with a layer of baking beads or rice. Chill for 15 minutes and then bake on the heated baking tray for 15 minutes. Remove the beads and paper, reduce the heat to 160°C (315°F/Gas 2–3) and bake for another 5 minutes. Sprinkle marzipan over the pastry base and bake for a further 5–10 minutes, or until golden. Leave in the tin to cool.

5 To make the custard cream, blend the custard powder with a little milk until smooth. Transfer to a pan and add the remaining milk, sour cream and sugar. Stir over medium heat for 5–7 minutes, or until thickened. Stir in the vanilla essence. (If you aren't using the custard cream immediately, lay plastic wrap on the surface to prevent a skin forming.)

6 Spread the warm custard cream evenly over the pastry case. Cut the prunes in half lengthways and arrange over the custard. Warm the redcurrant and muscat mixture and carefully spoon over the tart to cover it completely. Refrigerate for at least 2 hours to let the custard firm up before serving.

Grandma's Tip

This dish is best assembled on the same day as serving.

Tarte Tatin

Preparation time: 15 minutes
Total cooking time: 1 hour
*   10 minutes*
Serves 6

100 g (3½ oz) unsalted butter
¾ cup (185 g) sugar
6 large pink lady or fuji apples,
    peeled, cored and quartered
1 sheet puff pastry

1   Preheat the oven to 220°C
    (425°F/Gas 7). Lightly grease a
    23 cm (9 inch) shallow cake tin.
    Melt the butter in a frying pan,
    add the sugar and cook, stirring,
    over medium heat for 4–5
    minutes, or until the sugar starts
    to caramelise and turn brown.
    Continue to cook, stirring, until
    the caramel turns golden brown.

2   Add the apple to the pan and
    cook over low heat for 20–25
    minutes, or until it starts to turn
    golden brown. Carefully turn
    the apple over and cook the
    other side until evenly coloured.
    If much liquid comes out of the
    apple, increase the heat until it
    has evaporated – the caramel
    should be sticky rather than
    runny. Remove from the heat.
    Using tongs, arrange the hot
    apple in circles in the tin and
    pour the sauce over the top.

3   Place the pastry over the apple,
    tucking the edge down firmly
    with the end of a spoon. Bake
    for 30–35 minutes, or until
    the pastry is cooked. Leave for
    15 minutes before inverting
    onto a serving plate. Remove
    the paper before serving.

Grandma's Tip

*The moisture content of the different
apples varies quite a lot, which affects
the cooking time. Golden delicious,
pink lady and fuji are good to use
because they don't break down
during cooking.*

Little Lemon Tarts

Preparation time: 40 minutes
Total cooking time: 15 minutes
Makes 24

2 cups (250 g) plain
   (all-purpose) flour
125 g (4 oz) unsalted butter, chilled
   and cubed
2 teaspoons caster (berry) sugar
1 teaspoon finely grated lemon rind
1 egg yolk
2–3 tablespoons iced water

Filling
125 g (4 oz) cream cheese, softened
½ cup (125 g) caster (berry) sugar
2 egg yolks
2 tablespoons lemon juice
½ cup (125 ml) sweetened condensed
   milk

1 Preheat the oven to 180°C
(350°F/Gas 4). Lightly oil two
12-hole patty tins. Sift the flour
into a bowl. Rub in the butter
until the mixture resembles fine
breadcrumbs. Add the sugar,
rind, egg yolk and water and
mix with a knife, using a cutting
action, until the mixture forms
beads. Turn out onto a lightly
floured surface and gather into a
smooth ball. Wrap in plastic and
refrigerate for 10 minutes.

2 Beat the cream cheese, sugar and
egg yolks until smooth and
thickened. Add the lemon juice
and condensed milk and beat
together well.

3 Roll out the dough between two
sheets of baking paper until
3 mm (⅛ inch) thick. Cut into
rounds with a 7 cm (2¾ inch)
fluted round cutter and line the
patty tins. Lightly prick each
base several times with a fork
and bake for 10 minutes, or
until just starting to turn
golden. Spoon 2 teaspoons of
filling into each case, then bake
for another 5 minutes, or until
the filling has set. Cool slightly
before removing from the tins.

Peach Pie

*Preparation time: 35 minutes +
  20 minutes refrigeration*
Total cooking time: 1 hour
Serves 6

500 g (1 lb) sweet shortcrust pastry
2 × 825 g (1 lb 11 oz) cans peach
  slices, drained
½ cup (125 g) caster (berry) sugar
¼ cup (30 g) cornflour (cornstarch)
¼ teaspoon almond essence
20 g (¾ oz) unsalted butter, chopped
1 tablespoon milk
1 egg, lightly beaten
1 tablespoon caster (berry) sugar,
  to sprinkle

1 Roll out two-thirds of the dough between two sheets of baking paper until large enough to line an 18 cm (7 inch) pie tin, pressing it firmly into the side and trimming away the excess. Refrigerate for 20 minutes.

2 Preheat the oven to 200°C (400°F/Gas 6). Line the pastry with baking paper and spread with a layer of baking beads or rice. Bake for 10 minutes, remove the paper and beads and return to the oven for 5 minutes, until the base is dry and lightly golden. Allow to cool.

3 Mix the peaches, caster (berry) sugar, cornflour (cornstarch) and almond essence and spoon into the pastry shell. Dot with butter and moisten the edge with milk.

4 Roll out the remaining dough to a 25 cm (10 inch) square. Using a fluted pastry cutter, cut the pastry into ten strips, each 2.5 cm (1 inch) wide. Lay the strips in a lattice pattern over the filling. Press firmly on the edges and trim. Brush the lattice with egg and sprinkle with sugar. Bake for 10 minutes, reduce the oven to 180°C (350°F/Gas 4) and bake for 30 minutes, or until the top is golden.

Key Lime Pie

Preparation time: 25 minutes
Total cooking time: 25 minutes +
   2 hours refrigeration
Serves 8

125 g (4 oz) sweet wheatmeal
   (digestive) biscuits
90 g (3 oz) butter, melted
4 egg yolks
400 g (13 oz) can condensed milk
½ cup (125 ml) lime juice
2 teaspoons finely grated lime rind
1 cup (250 ml) thickened
   (whipping) cream
lime rind, to garnish

1 Finely crush the biscuits in a
   food processor for 30 seconds.

2 Transfer to a bowl, add the
   butter and mix thoroughly with
   the crumbs. Press into a 23 cm
   (9 inch) pie dish and refrigerate
   until firm. Preheat the oven to
   180°C (350°F/Gas 4).

3 Beat the yolks, condensed
   milk, lime juice and rind with
   electric beaters for 1 minute.
   Pour into the crust and smooth

the surface. Bake for 20–25
minutes, or until set.

4 Refrigerate the pie for 2 hours or
   until well chilled. Decorate with
   whipped cream and lime rind.

Mince Pies

Preparation time: 40 minutes +
 40 minutes refrigeration
Total cooking time: 25 minutes
Makes 24

2 cups (250 g) plain (all-purpose) flour
½ teaspoon ground cinnamon
125 g (4 oz) unsalted butter, chilled and
 cubed
1 teaspoon finely grated orange rind
¼ cup (30 g) icing sugar, sifted
1 egg yolk
3–4 tablespoons iced water

Filling

⅓ cup (60 g) raisins, chopped
⅓ cup (60 g) soft brown sugar
¼ cup (40 g) sultanas
¼ cup (45 g) mixed peel
1 tablespoon currants
1 tablespoon chopped
 blanched almonds
1 small Granny Smith apple, grated
1 teaspoon lemon juice
1 teaspoon finely grated lemon rind
1 teaspoon finely grated orange rind
½ teaspoon mixed spice
¼ teaspoon grated fresh ginger
pinch of ground nutmeg
25 g (¾ oz) unsalted butter, melted
1 tablespoon brandy

1 Sift the flour, cinnamon and
 ¼ teaspoon salt into a large bowl. Add
 the butter and rub it into the flour with
 your fingertips until it resembles fine
 breadcrumbs. Stir in the orange rind
 and icing sugar and mix. Make a well in
 the centre and add the egg yolk and
 water. Mix with a flat-bladed knife,
 using a cutting action, until the mixture
 comes together in beads, adding more
 water if necessary. Gather together, lift
 out onto a lightly floured work surface
 and press together into a disc, wrap in
 plastic and refrigerate for 20 minutes.
 Mix together all the filling ingredients.

2 Preheat the oven to 180°C (350°F/Gas
 4). Grease two 12-hole shallow patty
 tins. Roll out two-thirds of the pastry
 between two sheets of baking paper
 until 3 mm (⅛ inch) thick. Use an 8 cm
 (3 inch) round cutter to cut out rounds
 to line the 24 patty tins.

3 Divide the filling among the patty cases.
 Roll out the remaining pastry and cut
 out 12 rounds with a 7 cm (2¾ inch)
 cutter. Using a 2.5 cm (1 inch) star
 cutter, cut a star from the centre of each
 and use this small piece to top 12 of the
 pies. Use the outside part to top the
 other 12, pressing the edges together to
 seal. Refrigerate for 20 minutes.

4 Bake for 25 minutes, or until the
 pastry is golden. Leave in the tins for
 5 minutes before cooling on a wire
 rack. Dust with icing sugar to serve.

Grandma's Note

*Any extra fruit mince can be
stored in a sterilised jar in
a cool, dark place for up
to 3 months.*

Pumpkin Pie

*Preparation time: 20 minutes +
   40 minutes refrigeration + cooling*
*Total cooking time: 1 hour
   30 minutes*
Serves 6–8

1¼ cups (150 g) plain
   (all-purpose) flour
100 g (3½ oz) unsalted butter, chilled
   and cubed
2 teaspoons caster (berry) sugar
4 tablespoons iced water

Filling
750 g (1½ lb) butternut pumpkin
   (squash), cubed
2 eggs, lightly beaten
1 cup (185 g) soft brown sugar
⅓ cup (80 ml) cream
1 tablespoon sweet sherry or brandy
½ teaspoon ground ginger
½ teaspoon ground nutmeg
1 teaspoon ground cinnamon

1 Sift the flour into a large bowl
   and rub in the butter with your
   fingertips until the mixture
   resembles fine breadcrumbs.
   Mix in the caster (berry) sugar.
   Make a well in the centre, add
   almost all the water and mix
   with a flat-bladed knife, using a
   cutting action, until the mixture
   comes together in beads, adding
   more water if needed.

2 Gather the dough together and
   lift out onto a lightly floured
   work surface. Press into a disc.
   Wrap in plastic and refrigerate
   for 20 minutes.

3 Roll out the pastry between two
   sheets of baking paper until

large enough to line an 18 cm
(7 inch) pie dish. Line the dish
with pastry, trim away the excess
and crimp the edges with a fork.
Cover with plastic wrap and
refrigerate for 20 minutes.

4 Preheat the oven to 180°C
   (350°F/Gas 4). Cook the
   pumpkin (squash) in boiling
   water until tender. Drain, mash,
   push through a sieve and leave
   to cool.

5 Line the pastry shell with baking
   paper and spread with a layer of

baking beads or rice. Bake for
10 minutes, then remove the
paper and beads and bake for
10 minutes, or until lightly
golden. Set aside to cool.

6 Whisk the eggs and sugar together
   in a large bowl. Add the cooled
   pumpkin, cream, sherry and the
   spices and stir thoroughly. Pour
   into the pastry shell, smooth the
   surface and bake for 1 hour, or
   until set. If the pastry overbrowns,
   cover the edges with foil. Cool
   before serving.

Strawberry and Mascarpone Tart

Preparation time: 45 minutes +
45 minutes refrigeration
Total cooking time: 30 minutes
Serves 6

Pastry
1½ cups (185 g) plain (all-purpose)
flour
125 g (4 oz) unsalted butter, chilled
and cubed
⅓ cup (80 ml) iced water

Filling
500 g (1 lb) strawberries, hulled
and halved
2 teaspoons vanilla essence
50 ml (1½ fl oz) Drambuie
⅓ cup (60 g) soft brown sugar
250 g (8 oz) mascarpone
300 ml (10 fl oz) thickened
(whipping) cream
2 teaspoons finely grated orange rind

1 Sift the flour into a large bowl
and add the butter. Rub the
butter into the flour with your
fingertips until it resembles fine
breadcrumbs. Make a well in the
centre, add almost all the water
and mix with a flat-bladed knife,
using a cutting action, until the
mixture comes together in
beads, adding the remaining
water if needed. Gently gather
the dough together and lift out
onto a lightly floured surface.

2 Roll the dough out between two
sheets of baking paper until large
enough to line a lightly greased
23 cm (9 inch) loose-based tart

tin. Trim away the excess then
refrigerate the pastry-lined tin
for 15 minutes. Preheat the oven
to 200°C (400°F/Gas 6) and
heat up a baking tray in the oven.

3 Line the pastry with baking
paper and spread with a layer of
baking beads or rice. Bake on the
heated tray for 15 minutes.
Remove the paper and beads and
bake for 10–15 minutes, or until
dry and golden. Cool completely.

4 Mix together the strawberries,
vanilla, Drambuie and
1 tablespoon of the brown sugar

in a bowl. In another bowl, mix
the mascarpone, cream, orange
rind and remaining brown sugar.
Cover both bowls and refrigerate
for 30 minutes, tossing the
strawberries once or twice.

5 Whip half the mascarpone
cream until firm, then evenly
spoon it into the tart shell.
Drain the strawberries, reserving
the liquid. Pile the strawberries
onto the tart. Serve slices of tart
with a drizzle of the reserved
strawberry liquid and the
remaining mascarpone cream.

Cakes, Puddings & Muffins

Laughter is brightest in the place where the food is.

Irish proverb

Sour Cherry Cake

Preparation time: 10 minutes
Total cooking time: 50 minutes
Serves 8–10

125 g (4 oz) unsalted butter, softened
¾ cup (185 g) caster (berry) sugar
2 eggs, lightly beaten
½ cup (95 g) ground almonds
1 cup (125 g) self-raising flour
½ cup (60 g) plain (all-purpose) flour
½ cup (125 ml) milk
680 g (1 lb 6 oz) jar pitted morello
　cherries, well drained
icing sugar, to dust

1　Preheat the oven to 180°C
(350°F/Gas 4). Grease and flour
a 23 cm (9 inch) fluted baba tin,
shaking out any excess flour.
Beat the butter and sugar with
electric beaters until pale. Add
the beaten egg gradually, beating
well after each addition.

2　Stir in the ground almonds,
then fold in the sifted flours
alternately with the milk. Gently
fold in the cherries. Spoon the
mixture into the prepared tin
and smooth the surface. Bake
for 50 minutes, or until a skewer
comes out clean when inserted
into the centre of the cake.
Leave to cool in the tin for
10 minutes before turning out
onto a wire rack to cool. Dust
with icing sugar before serving.

Grandma's Note

This cake is best eaten on
the day it is made.

Classic Sponge

Preparation time: 20 minutes
Total cooking time: 25 minutes

75 g (2½ oz) plain (all-purpose) flour
150 g (5 oz) self-raising flour
6 eggs
220 g (7 oz) caster (berry) sugar
2 tablespoons boiling water

1   Preheat the oven to 180°C (350°F/Gas 4). Lightly grease two deep 22 cm (9 inch) round cake tins and line the bases with baking paper. Dust the tins lightly with a little extra flour, shaking off the excess.

2   Sift the flours three times onto baking paper. (To make a light textured sponge, you must sift the flour several times. Sifting not only removes any lumps in the flour but incorporates air.) Beat the eggs in a large mixing bowl with electric beaters for 7 minutes, or until thick and pale.

3   Gradually add the sugar to the eggs, beating well after each addition. Using a metal spoon, fold in the sifted flour and hot water. The secret to making the perfect sponge lies in the folding technique. A beating action, or using a wooden spoon, will cause loss of volume in the egg mixture and result in a flat, heavy cake.

4   Spread evenly into the prepared tins and bake for 25 minutes, or until the sponge is lightly golden and shrinks slightly from the side of the tin. Leave the sponges in their tins for 5 minutes before turning out onto a wire rack to cool completely.

5   Slice cake horizontally into as many layers as desired. Garnish with strawberries and sweetened cream.

Grandma's Notes

This sponge is best eaten on the day it is made. It won't keep well as it only contains a very small amount of fat.

Eggs should be at room temperature before adding them to the mixture. Take the eggs out of the fridge for at least an hour before required.

Triple Truffle Cake

*Preparation time: 1 hour 30 minutes +
45 minutes refrigeration*
*Total cooking time: 20 minutes + cake
cooking time*

Cake

A 22 cm (9 inch) round cake. We used
the mud cake on page 160.

Chocolate glaze

1⅔ cups (250 g) dark (semi-sweet)
   chocolate, chopped
½ cup (125 ml) cream
165 g (5½ oz) sugar

Truffles

300 g (10 oz) Madeira cake crumbs
2 tablespoons jam (jelly)
¼ cup (60 ml) cream
60 g (2 oz) unsalted butter, melted
2 cups (300 g) milk or dark (semi-sweet)
   chocolate, melted
2 tablespoons rum
1 cup (150 g) each of white, milk and dark
   (semi-sweet) compound chocolate
1 egg white
1–2 sheets 24 carat edible gold leaf

1 Cut the dome off the cake to give a
   flat surface. Turn the cake upside
   down on a rack and place over a tray
   to catch the glaze that runs over.

2 To make the glaze, put the chocolate,
   cream and sugar in a pan and stir
   over low heat until smooth. Bring to
   the boil, then reduce the heat and
   simmer for 4–5 minutes, stirring
   occasionally. Remove from the heat
   and stir gently, to cool a little.

3 Pour the glaze over the cake, letting
   it run evenly down the side. Tap the
   tray on the bench to level the
   surface. Leave to set completely.

4 Line a baking tray (sheet) with baking
   paper or foil. To make the truffles, mix
   together the cake crumbs, jam (jelly),
   cream, butter, melted chocolate and rum,
   stirring until moistened. Refrigerate
   for 20–30 minutes, or until firm. Roll
   teaspoons of the mixture into balls
   and place on the tray. Refrigerate for
   10–15 minutes, or until firm.

5 Line three trays with baking paper or
   foil. Place the white chocolate in a
   heatproof bowl. Bring a small pan of
   water to a simmer, remove from the heat
   and place the bowl over the pan, making
   sure it doesn't sit in the water. Stir the
   chocolate until melted. Repeat with the
   milk and dark (semi-sweet) chocolate.

6 Using a fork, dip the truffles in the
   different chocolates, tapping gently on
   the edge of the bowl to drain away the
   excess. Dip a third of the truffles in the
   white chocolate, a third in the milk
   and the rest in the dark. Leave on the
   baking trays to set. Make sure the
   chocolate is not too hot, or the truffles
   may melt and the chocolate discolour.
   If you find the chocolate too thick,
   melt and add 15 g (½ oz) Copha
   (white vegetable shortening).

7 Dab a spot of egg white onto
   the dark chocolate truffles,
   then remove the gold leaf
   from the sheet with
   tweezers and press
   onto the egg white.
   Put the cake on a
   serving plate and pile
   the truffles on top.

Grandma's Note

*The cake can be glazed up to a day in
advance. Pile with the truffles just prior to
serving (use a little melted chocolate to stick
them to the cake). The truffles can be kept
for 2–3 days in an airtight container
in a cool, dry place.*

Blueberry Cheesecake

Preparation time: 45 min +
  1 hour 30 minutes cooling
Total cooking time: 1 hour
Serves 8

150 g (5½ oz) plain (all-purpose) flour
1 tablespoon cocoa
100 g (3½ oz) butter, chopped
50 g (1¾ oz) sugar

Topping
4 eggs, separated
200 g (7 oz) sugar
1 kg (2 lb, 3 oz) quark (baking cheese)
1 lemon, juiced and zest grated
2 tablespoons cornflour (cornstarch)
2 tablespoons apricot jam (jelly)
400 g (14 oz) blueberries
icing sugar, to dust

1 Heat the oven to 200°C (400°F/Gas 6).

2 To make the base, mix together the flour and cocoa. Add the butter and knead quickly into a smooth dough. Cover in plastic wrap and chill for 30 minutes.

3 Place the mixture in a 24 cm (9½ in) cake tin lined with baking paper and pierce a few times with a fork.

4 To make the topping, beat the egg white and a pinch of salt until stiff peaks form. Mix together the egg yolks and the sugar until light and fluffy. Add the quark (baking cheese), lemon juice and zest to the egg yolk mixture.

5 Sift in the cornflour and then fold in the beaten egg white. Pour the mixture onto the dough and spread evenly. Bake for approximately 1 hour.

6 Remove from the oven and leave to cool in the tin, then remove the cake from the tin.

7 Heat the apricot jam with 2 tablespoons water and sift. Brush onto the cake. Place the blueberries on top of the cake and serve sprinkled with icing sugar.

Bread and Butter Pudding

Preparation time: 15 minutes +
*   45 minutes standing*
Total cooking time: 40 minutes
Serves 4

30 g (1 oz) butter
8 thick slices day-old bread
2 tablespoons sultanas
3 tablespoons caster (berry) sugar
1 teaspoon mixed spice
3 eggs, beaten
2 teaspoons vanilla essence

3 cups (700 ml) milk
½ cup (125 ml) cream
1 tablespoon demerara (light
    brown) sugar

1 Grease a 22 × 18 × 8 cm (9 ×
    7 × 3 inch) ovenproof dish.
    Butter the bread, cut in half
    diagonally and layer in the dish.
    Sprinkle the combined sultanas,
    sugar and mixed spice.

2 Whisk the eggs, vanilla, milk
    and cream and pour over the
    bread. Leave to stand for 45
    minutes, then top with the
    demerara (light brown) sugar.
    Preheat the oven to 180°C
    (350°F/Gas 4).

3 Bake for about 35–40 minutes,
    or until the custard around the
    bread has set. Serve hot.

Coffee Liqueur Gateau

Preparation time: 1 hour + 1 hour refrigeration
Total cooking time: 35–40 minutes
Serves 8–10

125 g (4 oz) brazil nuts
⅔ cup (100 g) blanched almonds
80 g (2¾ oz) hazelnuts
2 tablespoons plain (all-purpose) flour
¾ cup (185 g) caster (berry) sugar
7 egg whites
¼ cup (60 ml) Tia Maria or Kahlúa
small chocolate buttons, to decorate
sifted icing sugar, to dust

Coffee cream
200 g (6½ oz) butter
1 cup (150 g) dark (semi-sweet)
    chocolate, melted
2–3 teaspoons icing sugar
2 teaspoons warm water
3–4 teaspoons instant coffee powder

1 Preheat the oven to 180°C (350°F/ Gas 4). Lightly grease a deep 20 cm (8 inch) round tin and line base and side with baking paper. Place the nuts on a baking tray and roast for 5–10 minutes, or until golden. Rub the nuts vigorously in a clean tea towel to remove hazelnut skins. Place in a food processor and process until finely ground.

2 Transfer the ground nuts to a large bowl. Add the flour and 125 g (4 oz) of the sugar and mix well. Using electric beaters, beat the egg whites in a large mixing bowl until soft peaks form. Gradually add the remaining sugar, beating until the mixture is thick and glossy and the sugar is dissolved. Using a metal spoon, fold the nut mixture into the egg mixture a third at a time. Spoon into the prepared tin and smooth the surface. Bake for 35–40 minutes, or until springy to the touch. Leave in the tin to cool.

3 To make the coffee cream, beat the butter in a small mixing bowl with electric beaters until light and creamy. Gradually pour in the melted chocolate, beating until well combined. Add the icing sugar and combined water and coffee. Beat until smooth.

4 To assemble the gateau, turn the cake onto a flat working surface. Using a sharp serrated knife, carefully cut the cake horizontally into three layers. (Use the top layer of cake as the base of gateau.) Brush the first layer with half the liqueur. Spread with one fifth of the coffee cream.

5 Place the second cake layer on top. Brush with the remaining liqueur and spread with a quarter of the remaining coffee cream. Place the remaining layer on top. Spread top and sides with the remaining coffee cream.

6 Decorate with the chocolate buttons and dust with the icing sugar. Refrigerate for 1 hour or until firm.

Chocolate Mud Cake

Preparation time: 30 minutes
Total cooking time: 2 hours
Serves 8

250 g (8 oz) unsalted butter
250 g (8 oz) dark (semi-sweet)
  chocolate, chopped
2 tablespoons instant coffee powder
150 g (5 oz) self-raising flour
150 g (5 oz) plain (all-purpose) flour
½ teaspoon bicarbonate of soda
  (baking soda)
½ cup (60 g) cocoa powder
2¼ cups (550 g) caster (berry) sugar
4 eggs, lightly beaten
2 tablespoons oil
½ cup (125 ml) buttermilk

Icing

150 g (5 oz) unsalted butter, chopped
150 g (5 oz) dark (semi-sweet)
  chocolate, chopped

1 Preheat the oven to 160°C
(315°F/Gas 2–3). Lightly grease
a deep 22 cm (9 inch) round cake
tin and line with baking paper,
making sure the paper around
the side extends at least 5 cm
(2 inches) above the top edge.

2 Put the butter, chocolate and
coffee in a saucepan with ¾ cup
(185 ml) hot water and stir over
low heat until smooth. Remove
from the heat.

3 Sift the flours, bicarbonate of
soda (baking soda) and cocoa
powder into a mixing bowl. Stir
in the sugar and make a well in
the centre. Place the eggs, oil
and buttermilk in a separate
mixing bowl and mix until
combined. Pour into the dry
ingredients and mix together

with a whisk. Gradually add the
chocolate mixture, whisking
well after each addition.

4 Pour the mixture (it will be quite
wet) into the tin and bake for
1¾ hours. Test the centre with a
skewer – the skewer may be
slightly wetter than normal.
Remove the cake from the oven.
If the top looks raw, bake for
another 5–10 minutes, then
remove from oven. Leave in the
tin until completely cold, then
turn out and wrap in plastic wrap.

5 For the icing, combine the
butter and chocolate in a
saucepan and stir over low heat
until the butter and chocolate
are melted. Remove and cool
slightly. Pour over the cake and
allow it to run down the side.

Butter Cake

Preparation time: 20 minutes
Total cooking time: 1 hour
   15 minutes

280 g (9 oz) butter
225 g (7 oz) caster (berry) sugar
1½ teaspoons vanilla essence
4 eggs
225 g (7 oz) self-raising flour
150 g (5 oz) plain (all-purpose) flour
¾ cup (185 ml) milk

Grandma's Tip

This butter cake can be kept in an airtight container in the fridge for up to a week, or for 3–4 days in an airtight container in a cool dry place. It can be frozen for up to 2 months.

1 Preheat the oven to 180°C (350°F/Gas 4). Lightly grease a deep 20 cm (8 inch) round cake tin and line with baking paper.

2 Place the butter and sugar in a mixing bowl and beat with electric beaters until light and creamy. Add the vanilla essence then the eggs, one at a time, beating well after each addition.

3 Sift the flours together into a mixing bowl. Using a large metal spoon, add the combined sifted flours alternately with the milk into the butter mixture, folding until smooth. Spoon into the prepared tin and smooth the surface. Bake for 1¼ hours, or until a skewer comes out clean when inserted into the centre of the cake.

4 Leave the cake in the tin for at least 5 minutes before turning out onto a wire rack to cool completely.

5 Slice cake horizontally into as many layers as desired. Garnish with jam and sweetened cream or your favourite icing.

Pineapple Macadamia Cake

Preparation time: 10 minutes
Total cooking time: 1 hour
  15 minutes
Serves 10–12

3 cups (375 g) self-raising flour
1 teaspoon ground cinnamon
1½ cups (185 g) caster (berry) sugar
1 cup (90 g) desiccated (fine) coconut
5 eggs, lightly beaten
440 g (14 oz) can crushed pineapple
  in syrup
1½ cups (375 ml) vegetable oil
¾ cup (100 g) macadamia nuts, chopped

1   Preheat the oven to 180°C (350°F/
    Gas 4). Lightly grease a 23 cm (9 inch)
    round deep cake tin. Line the base and
    side with two sheets of baking paper,
    cutting it to make a collar that sits
    2–3 cm (¾–1 inch) above the side of
    the tin. Sift the flour and cinnamon
    into a bowl, add the sugar and coconut
    and stir to combine. Add the eggs,
    pineapple and oil and mix well. Stir in
    the macadamia nuts.

2   Spoon the mixture into the prepared tin
    and level the surface. Bake for 1 hour
    15 minutes, or until a skewer comes
    out clean when inserted into the centre
    of the cake. Cover the cake with oil if it
    browns too much. Leave in the tin for
    30 minutes before turning out onto a
    wire rack to cool completely.

3   Garnish with sweetened cream or your
    favourite icing.

Spiced Apple Sponge

Preparation time: 15 minutes
Total cooking time: 45 minutes
Serves 4

850 g (1 lb 14 oz) Granny
    Smith apples
30 g (1 oz) butter
⅓ cup (40 g) raisins
2 tablespoons lemon juice
4 cloves
1 cinnamon stick
pinch nutmeg
⅔ cup (160 g) caster (berry) sugar
2 eggs
finely grated zest of 1 lemon
¼ cup (30 g) self-raising flour
¼ cup (30 g) cornflour (cornstarch)
sifted icing sugar, to serve

1 Preheat the oven to 180°C (350°F/Gas 4). Peel, core and slice the apples into eighths. Melt the butter in a frying pan, add the apples and cook, stirring occasionally, over high heat for 7 minutes, or until browned. Add the raisins, juice, cloves, cinnamon, nutmeg, half the sugar and ½ cup (125 ml) water. Bring to the boil, then lower the heat and simmer for 3 minutes, or until the apples are tender. Remove the cinnamon stick and cloves. Spoon the apple mixture into a deep 8 cup (2 litre) round ovenproof dish.

2 To make the sponge topping, beat the eggs, remaining sugar and lemon zest in a small bowl with electric beaters for 7–8 minutes, or until the mixture is light and creamy. Fold in the sifted flours with a metal spoon.

3 Spoon the sponge topping over the apples. Bake in the oven for 30 minutes, or until the sponge is well risen and golden. Dust with icing sugar before serving. Suggested accompaniments include ice-cream, whipped cream (topping), hot or cold custard, sweetened ricotta cheese, and spiced mascarpone.

Butterfly Cupcakes

Preparation time: 10 minutes
Total cooking time: 30 minutes
Makes 12

125 g (4 oz) unsalted butter, softened
⅔ cup (160 g) caster (berry) sugar
1½ cups (185 g) self-raising flour
½ cup (125 ml) milk
2 eggs
½ cup (125 ml) whipped
   cream (topping)
¼ cup (80 g) strawberry jam (jelly)
icing sugar, to dust

1 Preheat the oven to 180°C (350°F/Gas 4). Line a flat-bottomed 12-hole cupcake tray with paper cases. Place the butter, sugar, flour, milk and eggs in a large mixing bowl. Using electric beaters, beat on low speed then increase the speed and beat until the mixture is smooth and pale. Divide the mixture evenly among the cases and bake for 30 minutes, or until cooked and golden. Transfer to a wire rack to cool.

2 Cut shallow rounds from the centre of each cake using the point of a sharp knife, then cut in half. Spoon 2 teaspoons of cream into each cavity, top with 1 teaspoon of jam (jelly) and position the two halves of the cake tops in the jam to resemble butterfly wings. Dust with icing sugar.

Grandma's Note

If using foil patty cases instead of the standard paper cases as suggested, the size and number of butterfly cakes may vary.

Rum Baba with Figs

Preparation time: 40 minutes +
  2 hours standing
Total cooking time: 35 minutes
Makes 10
Serves 4–6

1½ cups (185 g) plain
  (all-purpose) flour
2 teaspoons dried yeast
¼ teaspoon salt
2 teaspoons sugar
⅓ cup (80 ml) lukewarm milk
80 g (2¾ oz) butter
3 eggs, lightly beaten
2 cups (500 ml) water
1½ cups (375 g) caster (berry) sugar
⅓ cup (80 ml) dark rum
¾ cup (240 g) apricot jam (jelly)
2 tablespoons dark rum, extra
4–6 figs

1 Lightly brush ten ½-cup (125 ml)
   dariole moulds with oil. Place
   1 tablespoon of the flour and the yeast,
   salt, sugar and milk in a small bowl.
   Cover with plastic wrap and leave in a
   warm place for 10 minutes, or until
   the mixture is foamy. Using your
   fingertips, rub butter into the
   remaining flour in a large
   mixing bowl, until it resembles
   fine breadcrumbs.

2 Add the yeast mixture and eggs to the
   flour mixture. Beat with a spoon for 2
   minutes, until smooth and glossy. Scrape
   the mixture down the side of the bowl.
   Cover and leave in a warm place for
   1½ hours, until well risen.

3 Preheat the oven to 210°C (415°F/Gas
   6–7). Using a wooden spoon, beat the
   mixture again for 2 minutes. Divide the
   mixture evenly between prepared tins.

Set aside, covered with plastic wrap, for
another 30 minutes, until the dough is
well risen.

4 Bake for 20 minutes, or until golden
   brown. Meanwhile, combine the water
   and sugar in a medium saucepan. Stir
   over medium heat without boiling until
   the sugar has dissolved. Bring to the boil
   then reduce heat slightly and simmer,
   without stirring, for 15 minutes. Remove
   from heat, cool slightly and add the rum.

5 Turn out onto a wire rack placed over
   a shallow oven tray. Brush the warm
   babas liberally with warm rum syrup
   until they are well soaked. Strain excess
   syrup to remove any crumbs if
   necessary and reserve syrup.

6 Heat the jam (jelly) in a small
   saucepan or in the microwave and
   strain through a fine sieve. Add the
   extra rum, stir to combine and brush
   the warm jam all over the babas to
   glaze. To serve, place one or two babas
   on each plate, drizzle a pool of
   reserved syrup around them. Cut the
   figs in half and place on the plate
   beside the babas.

Grandma's Notes

Rum Babas are best served on the day they
are made.

If you do not have dariole or baba
moulds, use empty baked bean tins. The
130 g (4½ oz) size is best. Wash and
dry the tins thoroughly and
prepare as directed.

Sticky Date Pudding

Preparation time: 25 minutes +
* 15 minutes standing*
Total cooking time: 50 minutes
Serves 8

1 cup (185 g) chopped pitted dates
1 teaspoon bicarbonate of soda
   (baking soda)
90 g (3¼ oz) butter, softened
½ cup (115 g) soft brown sugar
2 eggs, lightly beaten
1 teaspoon vanilla essence
1½ cups (185 g) self-raising flour, sifted

Sauce

1 cup (230 g) soft brown sugar
1 cup (250 ml) cream
90 g (3¼ oz) butter
½ teaspoon vanilla essence

1 Preheat the oven to 180°C
   (350°F/Gas 4). Brush an 18 cm
   (7 inch) square cake tin with
   melted butter and line the base
   with baking paper. Put the dates
   and soda in a bowl and add 1 cup
   (250 ml) boiling water. Stir and
   leave for 15 minutes.

2 Using electric beaters, beat the
   butter and sugar until light
   and creamy. Beat in the eggs
   gradually. Add the vanilla
   essence. Fold in half of the flour
   then half of the date mixture.
   Stir in the remaining flour and
   dates, mixing well. Pour into
   the prepared tin and bake for

50 minutes, or until cooked
when tested with a skewer.
Leave in the tin to cool for
10 minutes before turning out.

3 To make the sauce, put all
   ingredients in a saucepan and
   bring to the boil while stirring.
   Reduce the heat and simmer
   for 5 minutes. Pour over the
   warm pudding.

Apple Crumble

Preparation time: 10 minutes
Total cooking time: 40 minutes
Serves 6

1 kg (2 lb 4 oz) green apples, peeled, cored and sliced
2 tablespoons caster (berry) sugar
¾ cup (90 g) plain (all-purpose) flour
1 teaspoon ground cinnamon
100 g (3½ oz) cold butter, chopped
½ cup (115 g) soft brown sugar
½ cup (50 g) rolled oats

1 Preheat the oven to 190°C (375°F/Gas 5). Brush a 5 cup (1.25 litre) shallow heatproof dish with melted butter. Put the apples in a bowl and add the caster (berry) sugar and 3 tablespoons water. Mix well.

2 Sift the flour and cinnamon into a bowl. With your fingertips, rub in the butter until the mixture resembles breadcrumbs.

Add the brown sugar and oats, and mix well.

3 Put the apples into the dish and sprinkle on the topping. Bake for 40 minutes, or until the apples are tender and the topping is golden. Sprinkle with cinnamon and serve.

Flourless Orange and Almond Cake

Preparation time: 15 minutes
Total cooking time: 1 hour 30 minutes
Serves 8

Cake

2 oranges
1½ cups (280 g) ground almonds
1 cup (250 g) caster (berry) sugar
1 teaspoon baking powder
1 teaspoon vanilla essence
1 teaspoon Cointreau
6 eggs, lightly beaten
icing sugar, to dust

Syrup

2 cups (500 ml) freshly squeezed and
  strained orange juice
¾ cup (185 g) caster (berry) sugar
¼ cup (60 ml) Sauternes (sweet white
  desert wine)

1 Wash the oranges well to remove any
   sprays or waxes. Place the whole
   oranges in a large saucepan, add
   enough water to cover them and place
   a small plate on top to keep the
   oranges submerged. Gradually bring
   the water to the boil, then reduce the
   heat and leave them to simmer for
   40 minutes, or until the oranges are
   very soft. Preheat the oven to 180°C
   (350°F/Gas 4). Place the cake tin on a
   sheet of baking paper and trace around
   the outside, then cut out the shape
   with a pair of scissors. Lightly grease
   the tin, then place the baking paper,
   pencil-side down, onto the base of the
   tin and smooth out any bubbles.

2 Cut each of the oranges into quarters
   and leave the pieces to cool. Remove

any pips, then place the oranges in the
bowl of a food processor and blend
until they form a very smooth pulp.
Add the ground almonds, caster
(berry) sugar, baking powder, vanilla
essence and Cointreau and, using the
pulse button, process until all of the
ingredients are combined. Add the egg
and process again until just combined—
take care not to over-process. Pour the
orange mixture into the prepared tin
and bake for 50 minutes, or until the
cake is firm and leaves the side of the
tin. Leave to cool completely in the
tin. Dust with icing sugar to serve.

3 To make the syrup, place the orange
   juice in a saucepan with the sugar and
   Sauternes (wine). Place the saucepan
   over a medium heat and stir until the
   sugar is dissolved. Reduce the heat and
   simmer for about 20 minutes, or until
   the liquid is reduced by half and has
   become slightly syrupy. Skim off any
   scum that forms on the surface as you
   go. The syrup will thicken further as it
   cools. Poke some random holes in the
   top of the cake to let the syrup absorb,
   or just drizzle the syrup over the cake
   before dusting with icing sugar
   and serving.

Grandma's Note

*This makes a great dessert cake
served with fruit and cream.*

Banana Muffins

Preparation time: 15 minutes
Total cooking time: 15 minutes
Makes 12

2 cups (250 g) self-raising flour
1 cup (75 g) oat bran
¾ cup (185 g) caster (berry) sugar
60 g (2 oz) butter, melted
¾ cup (185 ml) milk
2 eggs, lightly beaten
1 cup (240 g) mashed, ripe banana
  (2 medium bananas)

1 Preheat the oven to 210°C
   (415°F/Gas 6–7). Lightly grease
   a 12-hole muffin tin. Sift the
   flour into a large bowl and add
   the oat bran and the sugar.
   Make a well in the centre of the
   dry ingredients.

2 Combine the butter, milk, eggs
   and banana in a separate mixing
   bowl and add to the flour
   mixture all at once. Using a
   wooden spoon, stir until just
   mixed. (Do not overbeat; the
   batter should remain lumpy.)

3 Spoon the mixture into the
   prepared tin. Bake for 15
   minutes, or until puffed and
   brown. Transfer the muffins to a
   wire rack to cool completely.

Grandma's Tip

*For muffins with a difference, beat 100 g
(3½ oz) cream cheese, 2 tablespoons icing
sugar and 2 teaspoons lemon juice with
electric beaters until light and creamy.
Spread over the muffins and top with
dried banana slices.*

Blueberry Muffins

Preparation time: 20 minutes
Total cooking time: 20 minutes
Makes 12

3 cups (375 g) plain
  (all-purpose) flour
1 tablespoon baking powder
¾ cup (165 g) firmly packed soft
  brown sugar
125 g (4 oz) butter, melted
2 eggs, lightly beaten
1 cup (250 ml) milk
1⅓ cups (185 g) fresh or thawed
  frozen blueberries

1 Preheat the oven to 210°C
   (415°F/Gas 6–7). Lightly grease
   two 6-hole muffin tins. Sift the
   flour and baking powder into a
   large mixing bowl. Stir in the
   sugar and make a well in the
   centre of the dry ingredients.

2 In a separate mixing bowl, add
   the melted butter, eggs and milk
   and stir to combine. Add all at
   once to the flour mixture and
   fold until just combined. (Do
   not overmix, the batter should
   look quite lumpy.)

3 Fold in the blueberries. Spoon
   the batter into the prepared tin.
   Bake for 20 minutes, or until
   golden brown. Turn out onto a
   wire rack to cool.

Jam Roly Poly

Preparation time: 20 minutes
Total cooking time: 35 minutes
Serves 4

2 cups (250 g) self-raising flour, sifted
125 g (4¼ oz) butter, roughly chopped
2 tablespoons caster (berry) sugar
¼ cup (50 ml) milk
⅔ cup (210 g) raspberry jam (jelly)
1 tablespoon milk, extra

1 Preheat the oven to 180°C (350°F/Gas 4) and line a baking tray (sheet) with baking paper. Sift the flour into a bowl and add the butter. Using your fingertips, rub the butter into the flour until the mixture resembles fine breadcrumbs. Stir in the sugar.

2 Add the milk and ¼ cup (50 ml) water, and stir with a flat-bladed knife to form a dough. Turn the dough out onto a lightly floured surface and gather together.

3 On a large sheet of baking paper, roll out the dough into a thin rectangle, 33 cm (13 inches) long and 23 cm (9 inches) wide. Spread with the raspberry jam (jelly), leaving a narrow border around the edge.

4 Roll up lengthways like a Swiss roll and place on the tray seam-side down. Brush with the extra milk and cook in the oven for 35 minutes, or until golden. Leave to stand for a few minutes, then slice using a serrated knife. Serve warm with custard.

Rice Pudding

Preparation time: 10 minutes
Total cooking time: 2 hours
Serves 4

¼ cup (55 g) short-grain rice
1⅔ cups (410 ml) milk
1½ tablespoons caster (berry) sugar
¾ cup (185 ml) cream
¼ teaspoon vanilla essence
¼ teaspoon grated nutmeg
1 bay leaf

1 Preheat the oven to slow 150°C (300°F/Gas 2) and grease a 4 cup (1 litre) ovenproof dish. In a bowl, mix together the rice, milk, caster (berry) sugar, cream and vanilla essence, and pour into the greased dish. Dust the surface with the grated nutmeg and float the bay leaf on top.

2 Bake the rice pudding for 2 hours, by which time the rice should have absorbed most of the milk and will have become creamy in texture with a brown skin on top. Serve hot.

Grandma's Tip

Add grated lemon or orange rind to give a citrus flavour.

Lemon Cream Cake

Preparation time: 20 minutes
Total cooking time: 20 minutes
Makes 1

⅓ cup (40 g) cornflour (cornstarch)
⅓ cup (40 g) plain (all-purpose) flour
⅓ cup (40 g) self-raising flour
4 eggs
⅔ cup (160 g) caster (berry) sugar
2 teaspoons grated lemon rind

Lemon cream

1½ cups (375 ml) cream
⅓ cup lemon butter (curd)
½ cup (60 g) halved pecans

1 Preheat the oven to 180°C
   (350°F/Gas 4). Lightly grease
   two shallow 20 cm (8 inch)
   round cake tins and line bases
   with baking paper. Grease the
   baking paper. Dust tins lightly
   with flour and shake off excess.
   Sift the combined flours three
   times onto baking paper.

2 Using electric beaters, beat the
   eggs in a large mixing bowl for
   5 minutes, or until thick and pale.
   Add the sugar gradually, beating
   constantly until dissolved. Using
   a metal spoon, fold in the lemon
   rind and sifted flours quickly
   and lightly.

3 Spoon the mixture evenly into
   the prepared tins and smooth
   the tops. Bake for 20 minutes,
   or until lightly golden. Leave the
   cakes for 2 minutes in the tins
   before turning out onto a wire
   rack to cool completely.

4 To make the lemon cream, place
   the cream and lemon butter
   (curd) in a small mixing bowl.
   Using electric beaters, beat until
   soft peaks form. Cut each cake
   in half horizontally and place
   one layer on a serving plate.
   Using a flat-bladed knife, spread
   the cake layer with a quarter of

the lemon cream. Continue
layering with the remaining cake
and lemon cream, icing the top
of the cake with lemon cream
as well. Sprinkle with pecans
and serve.

Grandma's Tip

This cake is best eaten on the day of baking. It can be assembled several hours ahead and chilled.

Fruit Cake

*Preparation time: 30 minutes +
overnight soaking of fruit*
*Total cooking time: 3 hours
15 minutes*

500 g (1 lb) sultanas
375 g (12 oz) raisins, chopped
250 g (8 oz) currants
250 g (8 oz) glacé (glazed)
  cherries, quartered
1 cup (250 ml) brandy or rum, plus
  1 tablespoon to glaze
250 g (8 oz) butter
230 g (7½ oz) soft dark brown sugar
2 tablespoons apricot jam (jelly)
2 tablespoons treacle (molasses) or
  golden (corn) syrup
1 tablespoon grated lemon or
  orange rind
4 eggs
350 g (11 oz) plain
  (all-purpose) flour
1 teaspoon ground ginger
1 teaspoon mixed spice
1 teaspoon ground cinnamon

1 Put the fruit in a bowl with the
brandy and soak overnight.

2 Preheat the oven to 150°C
(300°F/Gas 2). Lightly grease a
deep 22 cm (9 inch) round cake
tin. Cut two strips of baking
paper long enough to fit around
the outside of the tin and wide
enough to come 5 cm (2 inches)
above the top of tin. Fold down
a cuff about 2 cm (1 inch) deep
along the length of each strip.
Make diagonal cuts up to the
fold line approximately 1 cm
(½ inch) apart. Fit the strips
around the inside of the tin,
pressing the cuts so that they

sit flat around the bottom edge
of the tin. Cut two circles of
baking paper, using the tin as
a guide, and line the base. Wrap
a folded piece of newspaper
around the outside of the tin
and tie securely with string.

3 Beat the butter and sugar in a
large bowl with electric beaters
until just combined. Beat in the
jam (jelly), treacle (molasses)
and rind. Add the eggs one at a
time, beating after each addition.

4 Stir the fruit and the combined
sifted flour and spices alternately
into the mixture.

5 Spoon into the prepared tin and
smooth the surface. Tap the tin
on the bench to remove any air
bubbles. Dip your hand in water
and level the surface. Sit the cake
tin on several layers of newspaper
in the oven and bake for 3 hours,
or until a skewer comes out clean
when inserted into the centre.
Brush with the extra tablespoon
of brandy. Cover the top of the
cake with paper and wrap in a tea
towel. Leave to cool completely
in the tin.

Grandma's Tip

*This cake can be kept, tightly wrapped
in plastic wrap, in a cool dry place for
up to 8 months or frozen for at
least 12 months.*

Strawberry Trifle

*Preparation time: 20 minutes +
4 hours refrigeration
Total cooking time: Nil
Serves 8*

2 × 85 g (3 oz) packets red jelly
  (jello) crystals
1 cup (250 ml) brandy or rum
1 cup (250 ml) milk
2 × 250 g (8 oz) packets thin
  sponge fingers
500 g (1 lb) strawberries, sliced
750 ml (24 fl oz) carton custard
1¼ cups (315 ml) whipped
  cream (topping)

1 Mix the jelly (jello) crystals with
1¾ cups (440 ml) of boiling water
and stir to dissolve. Pour into a
shallow tin and refrigerate until
the jelly has just set but is not firm.

2 Combine the brandy and milk
in a dish. Dip half the sponge
fingers in the brandy mixture
then place in a single layer in a
12 cup (3-litre) glass or ceramic
dish. Spoon half the jelly over
the sponge fingers. Scatter with
half the strawberries and then
half of the custard.

3 Dip the remaining sponge
fingers in the brandy mixture
and place evenly over the
custard, followed by the
remaining jelly and custard.
Spread the whipped cream
(topping) evenly over the
custard and top with the
remaining strawberries. Cover
and refrigerate for 4 hours
before serving.

Passionfruit and Lemon Curd Sponge

Preparation time: 1 hour
30 minutes
Total cooking time: 40 minutes +
cake cooking time

two 22 cm (9 inch) classic sponge
  cakes. We used the recipe on
  page 153.
50 g (1½ oz) white chocolate melts

Passionfruit topping
185 g (6 oz) passionfruit pulp
  (6–8 passionfruit)
3 tablespoons orange juice
2 tablespoons caster (berry) sugar
1 tablespoon cornflour (cornstarch)

Lemon cream
3 egg yolks
75 g (2½ oz) caster (berry) sugar
2 teaspoons finely grated lemon rind
90 ml (3 fl oz) lemon juice
180 g (6 oz) unsalted butter, chopped
300 ml (10 fl oz) thickened
  (whipping) cream

1 For the passionfruit topping,
   strain the passionfruit to
   separate the juice and seeds –
   you will need 125 ml (4 fl oz)
   passionfruit juice and 1½
   tablespoons of seeds. Put the
   passionfruit juice, seeds, orange
   juice and sugar in a small
   saucepan. In a separate bowl,
   mix the cornflour (cornstarch)
   with 3 tablespoons water until
   smooth and then add to the
   saucepan. Stir constantly over

medium heat until the mixture
boils and thickens, then pour
into a small bowl, lay a sheet
of plastic wrap directly on the
surface, and refrigerate until cold.

2 Bring a saucepan containing a
   little water to a simmer, then
   remove from the heat. Place the
   chocolate melts in a heatproof
   bowl, then place the bowl over
   the saucepan. Make sure the
   base of the bowl does not sit in
   the water. Stir the chocolate over
   the heat until it has completely
   melted. Spoon the chocolate
   into a paper piping bag and pipe
   lattice patterns onto a sheet of
   baking paper. Leave to set,
   then peel away the paper.

3 To make the lemon cream, put
   the yolks and sugar in a jug and
   beat well. Strain into a heatproof
   bowl and add the lemon rind,
   juice and butter. Place the bowl
   over a saucepan of simmering
   water, making sure the base
   does not touch the water. Stir
   constantly for 20 minutes, or
   until the mixture thickens
   enough to coat the back of a
   wooden spoon. Cool the lemon
   curd completely before folding
   into the cream. Beat until the
   mixture has the texture of thick
   sour cream.

4 Slice each cake in half
   horizontally and place one cake
   layer onto a serving plate.
   Spread with a quarter of the
   lemon cream, then top with
   another cake layer. Repeat with
   the remaining lemon cream and
   cake, finishing with a layer of
   lemon cream. Use a fork to
   roughly spread the cream.

5 Stir the passionfruit topping
   slightly to make it pourable
   and, if necessary, add a little
   orange juice to thin it. Pour
   the topping evenly over the
   cake, allowing it to run down
   the side. Stand the chocolate
   lattices on top.

Grandma's Note

*The lemon cream and passionfruit topping
can be stored for up to 3 days. Assemble the
cake an hour before serving, and don't pour
over the topping until ready to serve.*

Plum Cobbler

Preparation time: 25 minutes
Total cooking time: 35 minutes
Serves 6

750 g (1½ lb) plums
⅓ cup (90 g) sugar
1 teaspoon vanilla essence

Topping

1 cup (125 g) self-raising flour
60 g (2 oz) cold butter, chopped
¼ cup (55 g) firmly packed soft
   brown sugar
¼ cup (60 ml) milk
1 tablespoon caster (berry) sugar

1 Preheat the oven to moderately
hot 200°C (400°F/Gas 6). Cut
the plums into quarters and
remove the stones. Put the plums,
sugar and 2 tablespoons water
into a pan and bring to the boil,
stirring, until the sugar dissolves.

2 Reduce the heat, then cover and
simmer for 5 minutes, or until
the plums are tender. Remove
the skins from the plums if
desired. Add the vanilla essence
and spoon the mixture into a
3 cup (750 ml) ovenproof dish.

3 To make the topping, sift the
flour into a large bowl and add
the butter. Using your fingertips,
rub the butter into the flour
until it resembles fine
breadcrumbs. Stir in the brown
sugar and 2 tablespoons of milk.

4 Stir with a knife to form a soft
dough, adding more milk if
necessary. Turn the mixture out
onto a lightly floured surface
and gather together to form a
smooth dough. Roll out until
the dough is 1 cm (½ inch)
thick and cut into rounds using
a 4 cm (1½ inch) cutter.

5 Overlap the rounds around the
side of the dish over the filling.
(The plums in the middle will
not be covered.) Lightly brush
with milk and sprinkle with
sugar. Cook in the oven on a
baking tray for 30 minutes, or
until the topping is golden and
cooked through.

Grandma's Pavlova

Preparation time: 30 minutes
Total cooking time: 1 hour
Serves 6

4 egg whites
1 cup (250 g) caster (berry) sugar
2 teaspoons cornflour (cornstarch)
1 teaspoon white vinegar
2 cups (500 ml) cream
3 passionfruit
    strawberries, for decoration

1 Preheat the oven to 160°C
   (315°F/Gas 2–3). Line a 32 ×
   28 cm (12 × 11 inch) baking
   tray (sheet) with baking paper.

2 Put the egg whites and a pinch
   of salt in a small bowl. Using
   electric beaters, beat until stiff
   peaks form. Add the sugar
   gradually, beating constantly,
   until the sugar has dissolved and
   the mixture is glossy.

3 Using a metal spoon, fold in the
   cornflour (cornstarch) and
   vinegar. Spoon the mixture into
   a mound on the baking tray.
   Lightly flatten the top of the
   pavlova and smooth the sides.
   Bake for 1 hour, or until pale
   cream and crisp. Remove from
   the oven while warm and
   carefully turn upside down onto
   a plate. Allow to cool.

4 Lightly whip the cream until
   soft peaks form, and spread
   over the centre. Decorate
   with passionfruit pulp and
   strawberry halves.

Lemon Berry Cheesecake

Preparation time: 25 minutes +
overnight refrigeration
Total cooking time: Nil
Serves 12

60 g (2 oz) sweet wheatmeal (digestive)
    biscuits, finely crushed
30 g (1 oz) butter, melted
300 g (10 oz) ricotta
2 tablespoons caster (berry) sugar
2 × 130 g (4¼ oz) tubs low-fat fromage
    frais or light vanilla Fruche
2 × 130 g (4½ oz) tubs low-fat
    lemon fromage frais or light
    lemon Fruche
2 teaspoons finely grated lemon rind
2 tablespoons fresh lemon juice
1 tablespoon gelatine
2 egg whites
250 g (8 oz) strawberries, halved

1 Lightly oil and line the base and sides
   of a 20 cm (8 inch) diameter
   springform tin with plastic wrap.
   Combine the biscuit crumbs and
   butter in a small bowl and press evenly
   over the base of the tin. Refrigerate
   while making the filling.

2 Combine the ricotta and sugar in a
   food processor until smooth. Add all
   the fromage frais, the lemon rind and
   juice and mix well. Put ¼ cup (60 ml)
   water in a small bowl, sprinkle the
   gelatine in an even layer onto the
   surface and leave to go spongy. Bring a
   small pan of water to the boil, remove
   from the heat and put the gelatine
   bowl in the pan. The water should
   come halfway up the side of the bowl.
   Stir the gelatine until clear and
   dissolved, then cool slightly. Stir the
   gelatine mixture into the ricotta
   mixture, then transfer to a large
   bowl. Beat the egg whites until soft
   peaks form, then fold into the
   ricotta mixture.

3 Pour the mixture into the prepared tin
   and refrigerate for several hours or
   overnight, until set. Carefully remove
   from the tin by removing the side and
   gently easing the plastic from underneath.
   Decorate with the halved strawberries.

Apple Sago Pudding

Preparation time: 15 minutes
Total cooking time: 50 minutes
Serves 4

⅓ cup (90 g) caster (berry) sugar
½ cup (100 g) sago (or tapioca)
600 ml (20 fl oz) fat-reduced milk
⅓ cup (55 g) sultanas
1 teaspoon vanilla essence
pinch ground nutmeg
¼ teaspoon ground cinnamon
2 eggs, lightly beaten
3 small ripe apples (about 250 g/8 oz),
    peeled, cored and very thinly sliced
1 tablespoon soft brown sugar

1 Preheat the oven to moderate 180°C (350°F/Gas 4). Grease a 6 cup (1.5 litre) ceramic soufflé dish. Place the sugar, sago (or tapioca), milk, sultanas and ¼ teaspoon salt in a saucepan and heat, stirring often. Bring to the boil, then reduce the heat and simmer for 5 minutes.

2 Stir in the vanilla essence, nutmeg, cinnamon, egg and the apple slices, then pour into the prepared dish. Sprinkle with the brown sugar and bake for 45 minutes, or until set and golden brown.

Grandma's Note

If you prefer, you can use skim milk instead of fat-reduced milk.

Spotted Dick

Preparation time: 20 minutes
Total cooking time: 1 hour
   30 minutes
Serves 4

1½ cups (185 g) plain
  (all-purpose) flour
1½ teaspoons baking powder
½ cup (125 g) sugar
1½ teaspoons ground ginger
2 cups (160 g) fresh breadcrumbs
60 g (2¼ oz) sultanas
110 g (4 oz) currants
1½ cups (125 g) grated suet
2 teaspoons finely grated lemon zest
2 eggs, lightly beaten
⅔ cup (170 ml) milk

1 Sift the flour, baking powder,
sugar and ginger into a large
bowl. Add the breadcrumbs,
sultanas, currants, suet and
lemon zest. Mix thoroughly
with a wooden spoon.

2 Combine the egg and milk, and
add to the dry ingredients. Mix
together well, adding a little
more milk if necessary, then set
aside for 5 minutes. Lay a sheet
of baking paper on the work
surface and form the mixture
into a roll shape about 20 cm
(8 inches) long. Roll the pudding
in the paper and fold up the
ends (do not wrap it too tight as
it has to expand as it cooks).
Wrap the roll in a tea towel, put
it in the top of a bamboo steamer
over a wok filled one third full
of water. Cover and allow to
simmer for 1½ hours. Do not
let the pudding boil dry –
replenish with boiling water as
the pudding cooks. Unmould
the pudding onto a serving
plate, cut into slices and serve
with warm custard or cream.

Grandma's Note

Suet can be bought at good butchers, but as
they might have to get it in specially, order
it a few days before you need it. Store suet in
the freezer until ready to use – this makes
it much easier to grate.

Madeira Cake

Preparation time: 10 minutes
Total cooking time: 1 hour
Serves 6

180 g (6 oz) unsalted butter, softened
¾ cup (185 g) caster (berry) sugar
3 eggs, beaten
1⅓ cups (165 g) self-raising
    flour, sifted
2 teaspoons finely grated lemon rind
1 teaspoon lemon juice
2 teaspoons caster (berry) sugar,
    extra, to sprinkle
icing sugar, to dust
1 tablespoon lemon zest

1 Preheat the oven to 160°C
(315°F/Gas 2–3). Lightly grease
and flour a deep 18 cm (7 inch)
round cake tin, shaking out any
excess flour. Beat the butter and
sugar with electric beaters until
pale and creamy. Add the eggs
gradually, beating well after
each addition. Fold in the flour,
lemon rind and juice until
combined. When smooth,
spoon into the prepared tin
and level the surface.

2 Sprinkle the extra sugar over the
top. Bake for 1 hour, or until a
skewer comes out clean when
inserted into the centre of
the cake. Allow to cool for
15 minutes in the tin before
turning out onto a wire rack to
cool completely. If desired, dust
with icing sugar and garnish
with lemon zest.

Measurement Table

The recipes in this book were developed using a tablespoon measure of 20 ml. In some other countries the tablespoon is 15 ml. For most recipes this difference will not be noticeable but, for recipes using baking powder, gelatine, bicarbonate of soda, small amounts of flour and cornflour, we suggest that, if you are using the smaller tablespoon, you add an extra teaspoon for each tablespoon.

The recipes in this book are written using convenient cup measurements. You can buy special measuring cups in the supermarket or use an ordinary household cup: first you need to check it holds 250 ml (8 fl oz) by filling it with water and measuring the water (pour it into a measuring jug or even an empty yoghurt carton). This cup can then be used for both liquid and dry cup measurements.

Liquid cup measures		
¼ cup	60 ml	2 fluid oz
⅓ cup	80 ml	2½ fluid oz
½ cup	125 ml	4 fluid oz
¾ cup	180 ml	6 fluid oz
1 cup	250 ml	8 fluid oz

Spoon measures	
¼ teaspoon	1.25 ml
½ teaspoon	2.5 ml
1 teaspoon	5 ml
1 tablespoon	20 ml

Weight	
10 g	¼ oz
30 g	1 oz
60 g	2 oz
90 g	3 oz
125 g	4 oz
150 g	5 oz
185 g	6 oz
220 g	7 oz
250 g	8 oz
275 g	9 oz
300 g	10 oz
330 g	11 oz
375 g	12 oz
400 g	13 oz
425 g	14 oz
475 g	15 oz
500 g	1 lb
600 g	1¼ lb
650 g	1 lb 5 oz
750 g	1½ lb
1 kg	2 lb

Index

Almond Cinnamon Cookies	92
Anzac Biscuits	110
Apple Crumble	169
Apple Pie	126
Apple Sago Pudding	186
Bacon and Egg Pie	65
Bacon and Onion Rosti Cake	18
Banana Muffins	172
Banoffie Pie	139
Basic Shortbread Fingers	101
Beef and Caramelised Onion Pie	46
Beef Casserole with Caraway Dumplings	30
Beef Pot Roast	21
Beef, Stout and Potato Pie	53
Blackberry Pie	138
Blueberry Cheesecake	156
Blueberry Muffins	173
Bramble Pie	127
Bread and Butter Pudding	157
Bubble and Squeak	17
Butter Cake	161
Butterfly Cupcakes	165
Cabbage and Ham Soup with Cheese Dumplings	82
Cauliflower Cheese	23
Cheese and Onion Pie	42
Cherry Pie	130
Cherry Slice	98

Chicken and Corn Soup	73
Chicken and Leek Pie	44
Chicken and Mushroom Casserole	28
Chicken and Vegetable Soup	76
Choc-Mint Swirls	105
Chocolate Caramel Slice	121
Chocolate Carrot Slice	122
Chocolate Chip Cookies	117
Chocolate Mud Cake	160
Chunky Vegetable Soup	84
Clam Chowder	86
Classic Sponge	153
Coconut Macaroons	114
Coffee Liqueur Gateau	158
Corned Beef	34
Cornish Pasties	61
Cottage Pie	29
Country Lentil, Bacon and Garlic Soup	72
Cream of Mushroom Soup	81
Cream of Tomato Soup	68
Date and Peach Slice	99
Family-Style Meat Pie	52
Fisherman's Pie	25
Flourless Orange and Almond Cake	170
French Onion Soup	88
Fruit Cake	178
Fruity Shortbread Pillows	112

Game Pie	40	Moist Chocolate Brownies	118
Gingerbread People	100	Mulligatawny Soup	85
Gingernuts	116		
Grandma's Pavlova	183	Oxtail Soup	79
Ham and Chicken Pie	43	Passionfruit and Lemon Curd Sponge	180
		Passionfruit Shortbread	102
Jam Drops	104	Pea and Ham Soup	75
Jam Roly Poly	174	Peach Pie	144
		Pear and Almond Flan	137
Key Lime Pie	145	Pear and Pecan Pie	128
		Pecan Pie	131
Lamb Shank Pie	48	Picnic Pork Pies	50
Lamb's Liver and Bacon	27	Pineapple Macadamia Cake	162
Lancashire Hotpot	32	Plain Scones	93
Lebkuchen	106	Plum Cobbler	182
Leek and Potato Soup	69	Plum Pie	133
Lemon Berry Cheesecake	184	Potato and Carrot Soup	80
Lemon Cream Cake	177	Prune and Almond Custard Tart	140
Lemon Meringue Pie	132	Pumpkin Pie	148
Little Lemon Tarts	143	Pumpkin Scones	95
Madeira Cake	188	Quiche Lorraine	57
Marzipan Swirls	115		
Meat Loaf	33	Rabbit Pie	49
Meatballs in Tomato Sauce	26	Raised Pork Pie	54
Mince Pies	146	Raspberry Coconut Cookies	96
Minestrone	78	Raspberry Shortcake	108

Rhubarb Pie	134	Spotted Dick	187
Rice Pudding	176	Spring Vegetable Soup	89
Rich Beef Pie	62	Steak and Kidney Pie	60
Roast Chicken with Breadcrumb Stuffing	9	Steak and Kidney Pudding	35
Roast Leg of Pork	13	Sticky Date Pudding	168
Roast Potatoes with Rosemary	12	Strawberry and Mascarpone Tart	149
Roast Pumpkin Soup	70	Strawberry Trifle	179
Roast Vegetable Mash	10	Sultana Scones	94
Rosemary Lamb Cobbler	38	Summer Berry Tart	136
Rosemary-Infused Lamb-and-Lentil Casserole	20		
Rum Baba with Figs	166	Tarte Tatin	142
Rustic Hotpot	24	Toad in the Hole	15
		Tomato and Bacon Quiche	56
Salmon Fishcakes	22	Tomato and Thyme Quiche	58
Sausages and Mash with Onion Gravy	16	Traditional Roast Beef with Yorkshire Puddings	8
Scotch Broth	74	Triple Truffle Cake	154
Shepherd's Pie	14		
Shortbread Stars with Lemon Glaze	111	Vanilla Custard Kisses	109
Spiced Apple Sponge	164	Vegetable Lattice Pie	47
Smoked Haddock Chowder	87		
Sour Cherry Cake	152	Walnut Brownies	120
Spinach Pie	64		